MAJOR WORLD LEADERS

Vicente Fox

Sherry Beck Paprocki

CHELSEA HOUSE
PUBLISHERS
A Haights Cross Communications Company

Philadelphia

CHELSEA HOUSE PUBLISHERS

EDITOR IN CHIEF Sally Cheney
DIRECTOR OF PRODUCTION Kim Shinners
CREATIVE MANAGER Takeshi Takahashi
MANUFACTURING MANAGER Diann Grasse

Staff for VICENTE FOX

EDITOR Lee Marcott
ASSOCIATE EDITOR Ben Kim
PRODUCTION ASSISTANT Jaimie Winkler
PICTURE RESEARCH 21st Century Publishing and Communications, Inc.
SERIES DESIGNER Takeshi Takahashi
COVER DESIGNER Keith Trego
LAYOUT 21st Century Publishing and Communications, Inc.

A Haights Cross Communications ↗ Company

http://www.chelseahouse.com

First Printing

1 3 5 7 9 8 6 4 2

Library of Congress Cataloging-in-Publication Data applied for.

Paprocki, Sherry.
  Vicente Fox / Sherry Beck Paprocki.
    p. cm.—(Major world leaders)
Includes index.
  ISBN 0-7910-6944-3
  1. Fox Quesada, Vicente—Juvenile literature. 2. Mexico—Politics and government—
1988– —Juvenile literature. 3. Presidents—Mexico—Biography—Juvenile literature.
I. Title. II. Series.
F1236.6.F69 P36 2002
972.08'3'092—dc21

                                                                    2002008256

TABLE OF CONTENTS

J-B
FOX QUESADA
294-3044

On Leadership

Arthur M. Schlesinger, jr.

Leadership, it may be said, is really what makes the world go round. Love no doubt smoothes the passage; but love is a private transaction between consenting adults. Leadership is a public transaction with history. The idea of leadership affirms the capacity of individuals to move, inspire, and mobilize masses of people so that they act together in pursuit of an end. Sometimes leadership serves good purposes, sometimes bad; but whether the end is benign or evil, great leaders are those men and women who leave their personal stamp on history.

Now, the very concept of leadership implies the proposition that individuals can make a difference. This proposition has never been universally accepted. From classical times to the present day, eminent thinkers have regarded individuals as no more than the agents and pawns of larger forces, whether the gods and goddesses of the ancient world or, in the modern era, race, class, nation, the dialectic, the will of the people, the spirit of the times, history itself. Against such forces, the individual dwindles into insignificance.

So contends the thesis of historical determinism. Tolstoy's great novel *War and Peace* offers a famous statement of the case. Why, Tolstoy asked, did millions of men in the Napoleonic Wars, denying their human feelings and their common sense, move back and forth across Europe slaughtering their fellows? "The war," Tolstoy answered, "was bound to happen simply because it was bound to happen." All prior history determined it. As for leaders, they, Tolstoy said, "are but the labels that serve to give a name to an end and, like labels, they have the least possible connection with the event." The greater the leader, "the more conspicuous the inevitability and the predestination of every act he commits." The leader, said Tolstoy, is "the slave of history."

Determinism takes many forms. Marxism is the determinism of class. Nazism the determinism of race. But the idea of men and women as the slaves of history runs athwart the deepest human instincts. Rigid determinism abolishes the idea of human freedom—the assumption of free choice that underlies every move we make, every word we speak, every thought we think. It abolishes the idea of human responsibility,

since it is manifestly unfair to reward or punish people for actions that are by definition beyond their control. No one can live consistently by any deterministic creed. The Marxist states prove this themselves by their extreme susceptibility to the cult of leadership.

More than that, history refutes the idea that individuals make no difference. In December 1931 a British politician crossing Fifth Avenue in New York City between 76th and 77th Streets around 10:30 P.M. looked in the wrong direction and was knocked down by an automobile—a moment, he later recalled, of a man aghast, a world aglare: "I do not understand why I was not broken like an eggshell or squashed like a gooseberry." Fourteen months later an American politician, sitting in an open car in Miami, Florida, was fired on by an assassin; the man beside him was hit. Those who believe that individuals make no difference to history might well ponder whether the next two decades would have been the same had Mario Constasino's car killed Winston Churchill in 1931 and Giuseppe Zangara's bullet killed Franklin Roosevelt in 1933. Suppose, in addition, that Lenin had died of typhus in Siberia in 1895 and that Hitler had been killed on the western front in 1916. What would the 20th century have looked like now?

For better or for worse, individuals do make a difference. "The notion that a people can run itself and its affairs anonymously," wrote the philosopher William James, "is now well known to be the silliest of absurdities. Mankind does nothing save through initiatives on the part of inventors, great or small, and imitation by the rest of us—these are the sole factors in human progress. Individuals of genius show the way, and set the patterns, which common people then adopt and follow."

Leadership, James suggests, means leadership in thought as well as in action. In the long run, leaders in thought may well make the greater difference to the world. "The ideas of economists and political philoso-phers, both when they are right and when they are wrong," wrote John Maynard Keynes, "are more powerful than is commonly understood. Indeed the world is ruled by little else. Practical men, who believe them-selves to be quite exempt from any intellectual influences, are usually the slaves of some defunct economist. . . . The power of vested interests is vastly exaggerated compared with the gradual encroachment of ideas."

But, as Woodrow Wilson once said, "Those only are leaders of men, in the general eye, who lead in action. . . . It is at their hands that new thought gets its translation into the crude language of deeds." Leaders in thought often invent in solitude and obscurity, leaving to later generations the tasks of imitation. Leaders in action—the leaders portrayed in this series—have to be effective in their own time.

And they cannot be effective by themselves. They must act in response to the rhythms of their age. Their genius must be adapted, in a phrase from William James, "to the receptivities of the moment." Leaders are useless without followers. "There goes the mob," said the French politician, hearing a clamor in the streets. "I am their leader. I must follow them." Great leaders turn the inchoate emotions of the mob to purposes of their own. They seize on the opportunities of their time, the hopes, fears, frustrations, crises, potentialities. They succeed when events have prepared the way for them, when the community is awaiting to be aroused, when they can provide the clarifying and organizing ideas. Leadership completes the circuit between the individual and the mass and thereby alters history.

It may alter history for better or for worse. Leaders have been responsible for the most extravagant follies and most monstrous crimes that have beset suffering humanity. They have also been vital in such gains as humanity has made in individual freedom, religious and racial tolerance, social justice, and respect for human rights.

There is no sure way to tell in advance who is going to lead for good and who for evil. But a glance at the gallery of men and women in MAJOR WORLD LEADERS suggests some useful tests.

One test is this: Do leaders lead by force or by persuasion? By command or by consent? Through most of history leadership was exercised by the divine right of authority. The duty of followers was to defer and to obey. "Theirs not to reason why/Theirs but to do and die." On occasion, as with the so-called enlightened despots of the 18th century in Europe, absolutist leadership was animated by humane purposes. More often, absolutism nourished the passion for domination, land, gold, and conquest and resulted in tyranny.

The great revolution of modern times has been the revolution of equality. "Perhaps no form of government," wrote the British historian James Bryce in his study of the United States, *The American Commonwealth*, "needs great leaders so much as democracy." The idea that all people should be equal in their legal condition has undermined the old structure of authority, hierarchy, and deference. The revolution of equality has had two contrary effects on the nature of leadership. For equality, as Alexis de Tocqueville pointed out in his great study *Democracy in America,* might mean equality in servitude as well as equality in freedom.

"I know of only two methods of establishing equality in the political world," Tocqueville wrote. "Rights must be given to every citizen, or none at all to anyone . . . save one, who is the master of all." There was no middle ground "between the sovereignty of all and the absolute power of one man." In his astonishing prediction of 20th-century totalitarian dictatorship, Tocqueville explained how the revolution of equality could lead to the *Führerprinzip* and more terrible absolutism than the world had ever known.

But when rights are given to every citizen and the sovereignty of all is established, the problem of leadership takes a new form, becomes more exacting than ever before. It is easy to issue commands and enforce them by the rope and the stake, the concentration camp and the *gulag.* It is much harder to use argument and achievement to overcome opposition and win consent. The Founding Fathers of the United States understood the difficulty. They believed that history had given them the opportunity to decide, as Alexander Hamilton wrote in the first Federalist Paper, whether men are indeed capable of basing government on "reflection and choice, or whether they are forever destined to depend . . . on accident and force."

Government by reflection and choice called for a new style of leadership and a new quality of followership. It required leaders to be responsive to popular concerns, and it required followers to be active and informed participants in the process. Democracy does not eliminate emotion from politics; sometimes it fosters demagoguery; but it is confident that, as the greatest of democratic leaders put it, you cannot fool all of the people all of the time. It measures leadership by results and retires those who overreach or falter or fail.

It is true that in the long run despots are measured by results too. But they can postpone the day of judgment, sometimes indefinitely, and in the meantime they can do infinite harm. It is also true that democracy is no guarantee of virtue and intelligence in government, for the voice of the people is not necessarily the voice of God. But democracy, by assuring the right of opposition, offers built-in resistance to the evils inherent in absolutism. As the theologian Reinhold Niebuhr summed it up, "Man's capacity for justice makes democracy possible, but man's inclination to justice makes democracy necessary."

A second test for leadership is the end for which power is sought. When leaders have as their goal the supremacy of a master race or the promotion of totalitarian revolution or the acquisition and exploitation of colonies or the protection of greed and privilege or the preservation of personal power, it is likely that their leadership will do little to advance the cause of humanity. When their goal is the abolition of slavery, the liberation of women, the enlargement of opportunity for the poor and powerless, the extension of equal rights to racial minorities, the defense of the freedoms of expression and opposition, it is likely that their leadership will increase the sum of human liberty and welfare.

Leaders have done great harm to the world. They have also conferred great benefits. You will find both sorts in this series. Even "good" leaders must be regarded with a certain wariness. Leaders are not demigods; they put on their trousers one leg after another just like ordinary mortals. No leader is infallible, and every leader needs to be reminded of this at regular intervals. Irreverence irritates leaders but is their salvation. Unquestioning submission corrupts leaders and demeans followers. Making a cult of a leader is always a mistake. Fortunately hero worship generates its own antidote. "Every hero," said Emerson, "becomes a bore at last."

The signal benefit the great leaders confer is to embolden the rest of us to live according to our own best selves, to be active, insistent, and resolute in affirming our own sense of things. For great leaders attest to the reality of human freedom against the supposed inevitabilities of history. And they attest to the wisdom and power that may lie within the most unlikely of us, which is why Abraham Lincoln remains the supreme example of great leadership. A great leader, said Emerson, exhibits new possibilities to all humanity. "We feed on genius . . . . Great men exist that there may be greater men."

Great leaders, in short, justify themselves by emancipating and empowering their followers. So humanity struggles to master its destiny, remembering with Alexis de Tocqueville: "It is true that around every man a fatal circle is traced beyond which he cannot pass; but within the wide verge of that circle he is powerful and free; as it is with man, so with communities." ■

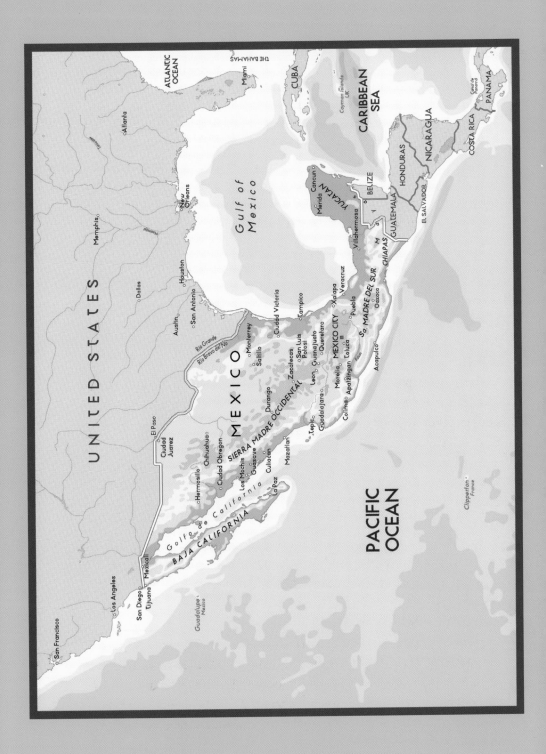

Newly elected President Vicente Fox, right, celebrates with his daughter, Cristina, on July 2, 2000. Francisco Labastida, the presidential candidate for the Institutional Revolutionary Party, had just conceded, making Fox the first opposition leader of Mexico in 71 years.

A Big Win

The Mexican crowd loudly cheered when they saw their new president emerge onto the balcony of his political party's headquarters. "Vicente Presidente," they shouted to him.

"I like it when you call me that," responded Vicente Fox, the opposition candidate who had just been voted president of Mexico during one of the most peaceful elections in the country's history.

It was July 2, 2000. Cars honked their horns and people poured into the streets of Mexico City to celebrate the country's new president. Some streets closed down as Fox made his way to the Angel of Independence, a well-known public statue in Mexico where soccer victories and other national events are celebrated, to make his first public speech. When he arrived, his supporters were wearing fake mustaches in a tribute to their favorite mustachioed politician. One man even wore a Vicente Fox mask.

"I extend my hand to everyone, to all the political parties, to all Mexicans. Today and in the future, we have to unite," Fox said.

The people of Mexico liked Fox because he was down to earth. He seemed to understand them and what the country needed. They liked his relaxed campaign style, the blue jeans and cowboy boots that he regularly wore and the casual shirts that he left unbuttoned at the neck. As though most people would not recognize him, he wore his surname on his silver belt buckle. But it was Vicente Fox's height that really set him apart. At nearly six and a half feet tall, he towered over the crowds along his campaign trail as he greeted those who came to see him. Sometimes he even campaigned through the countryside on horseback. All the while, he promised Mexicans that he could make their country better. He said he would eliminate police corruption, improve education, improve Mexico's economy while creating better jobs for residents, and take better care of the Mexican people.

"Today, we have proven that our democracy is a mature democracy," said outgoing Mexican President Ernesto Zedillo when he announced Fox's victory on television at 11 P.M. the night of July 2.

Widespread corruption and mismanagement of government issues have plagued Mexico for decades. But during President Zedillo's leadership in Mexico, prior to Fox's election, the country experienced a reformation in its election practices. Political campaign funding was made more equitable and the independent Federal Electoral Institute was created to oversee elections in the country. The election of July 2, 2000, was the first time in Mexico's history that the election was considered to be fair. In the past, the government had been accused of cheating during elections to ensure that the ruling party's candidate won. Some voters on this day said they thought it was the first time that the country's direction was really up to them. They had confidence that the Federal Electoral Institute would not rig the process.

Mexico is a country that has long been in turmoil, first ruled by the ancient Mayans, later joined by the pyramid-building Toltecs, and eventually, by the Aztecs. In 1519 a Spanish explorer named Hernán Cortés arrived and conquered the Aztec lands. For the following three hundred years, Mexico was a part of the Spanish Empire and went by the name of New Spain. Mexico gained its independence from Spain in 1821, but lost some of its lands when Texas broke away to join the United States, leading to a war between Mexico and the United States from 1846 to 1848. Mexico also lost California, New Mexico, and Arizona during that period.

The Mexican Revolution, from 1910 to about 1920, aimed to reduce the power of the Catholic Church, which was brought to Mexico by the Spaniards several centuries earlier. The revolution also sought to obtain land for the peasants who lived in poverty and to develop the country to benefit its people rather than foreigners who were interested in its wealth of resources, which included gold, silver, and oil. A new constitution was written on Feb. 5, 1917, that promised a reformation of the government. Mexico's constitution calls it the United Mexican States, a federal republic that consists of 31 states and the federal district, similar to the makeup of the United States government.

The main accomplishment of the Mexican Revolution was that it ended the bloody revolts that had riveted Mexico for centuries. The constitution created a system in which elections would be held every four years, with no ruler able to seek reelection. At the same time, the Party of the Mexican Revolution was created that eventually evolved into the prominent Institutional Revolutionary Party, or PRI. Mexico then began being governed by a new generation of people. Eventually, the constitution was changed to allow a president to stay in office for six years.

The creation of the PRI meant that there would be peaceful change from one ruler to another. But there were problems with this type of leadership. The result was that only one set of political beliefs controlled the country for the next 71 years. Even though members from other political parties ran for offices, such as governors in Mexican states, few were elected. Mexico was ruled, essentially, by dictatorship. Even though the president of the country changed, the same set of political beliefs followed. This type of government protected the ruling class, but many other people remained poor and uneducated.

Although Mexico is now one of the largest oil producers in the world, about half the country's population still lives in poverty. Some Mexicans earn as little as $2 a day for their work. During the election of 2000, nearly 58.8 million voters were given the opportunity to elect a new president, one who would fuel their desires for better government. Fox was a member of the National Action Party (PAN) and it was the first time in 71 years that anyone had won over candidates from Mexico's PRI.

Millions of Mexicans flocked to the voting polls that day, including those who lived and worked across the border in the United States. Special polling places were set up near the United States border for Mexicans who worked in the U.S. They traveled from as far away as Nevada and Washington state to take part in the exciting election for the Mexican president. Many Mexicans were happy to have the opportunity to elect a new president, who seemed honest and who cared about them. They were tired of being ruled by the PRI party.

Vicente Fox is the second of nine children born to a prosperous landowner, José Luis Fox, in the central state of Guanajuato. His mother, Mercedes Quesada, was born in

Tzotzil Indian women line up to cast their ballots in Mexico's presidential election, Sunday, July 2, 2000, in Chenalho, in the state of Chiapas. Despite the wealth that has come from Mexican oil, half of Mexico's population still lives in poverty. Many voters saw the 2000 election as a chance of a better life through new government.

Spain and immigrated to Mexico. When Fox was a young boy any dreams of being Mexico's president would have been squelched because a law forbade the children of immigrants from serving as president. But that law in the Mexican Constitution was amended in 1993, enabling Vicente the opportunity of a lifetime.

Vicente Fox grew up on a 1,100-acre ranch in San Francisco del Rincon. His father's father, who was a native of Ireland, had purchased the property during the Mexican Revolution. Fox attended a Jesuit school during secondary school that was in Guanajuato and later studied business at Mexico City's Ibero-American University. In 1964 he started his career as a route manager for Coca-Cola and later became the president for Coke in Mexico and Latin America, the youngest person in such a position.

When Coke offered him a promotion, which would have required him to move to the United States, Fox quit. He returned to his native Guanajuato where he worked with two of his brothers managing a large vegetable farm and the family's boot factories. He became that state's governor in 1995 and announced his intentions to run for president of the country two years later.

The night that Vicente Fox won the presidency, festive celebrations broke out throughout Mexico. It was the first time in history that an opposition candidate had been elected in Mexico without a violent rebellion.

"The citizens have made a decision that we should respect, and I'll set that example myself," said Fox's main opponent, PRI candidate Francisco Labastida. A third candidate, Cuauhtemoc Cárdenas, represented the Party for the Democratic Revolution (PRD). When the votes were tallied, Fox had easily won. He had received 40 percent of the vote, Labastida had received 35 percent, and Cárdenas, 19 percent.

In Mexico it was risky business to be a part of a political party that opposed the PRI. For decades, some candidates in the PAN would hang their posters at night to avoid the police. They feared for their lives if they did not agree with the PRI. But starting about 20 years ago, PAN candidates gradually began to take leadership roles in Mexico. When Fox was elected, seven governors were PAN members and 300 mayors, many in major Mexican cities, belonged to PAN.

By 8 P.M. on election night, Fox's supporters began gathering outside PAN's national headquarters in Mexico City. When the announcement of Fox's victory came a few hours later, the candidate was relieved and happy. He had received the support from Mexico's middle and upper classes. Also supporting him were those who were more educated, lived in the highly populated cities, and were young voters. But even many rural voters chose Fox as their leader.

"We are making this change and this transition without turbulence or anxiety," said Fox, in a nationally-televised statement on election night. His four adopted children stood behind him, but he was legally separated from his wife. Even though the crowds were jubilant that evening, Mexico's new president knew there was much work to be done. He would need to design a plan that was focused on reforming the government which had been ruled by the PRI party for so long.

"I have a lot of responsibility on my shoulders," he said. "I will not fail."

But this was a night for celebration. Mexicans were jubilant about the prospect of a real democracy in their country. In Tijuana, a Mexican city that sits only 20 minutes outside of San Diego, California, carloads of young people and families hit the streets forming parades along the city's main thoroughfares.

In the northern industrial city of Monterrey, the enthusiasm for Fox's election was widespread. More than 50,000 people gathered in one of the city's main plazas, celebrating Fox's victory and the defeat of the PRI. Back in Mexico City, the main plaza, Zocalo, shook with festivity as people praised Fox's election. Fox told the crowd that gathered at the angel: "There is so much to celebrate tonight." He continued by thanking the voters and his opponents for

Vicente Fox waves to thousands of supporters early on July 3, 2000, after winning the election in Mexico City. Fox promised that the departure from seven decades of single-party rule would mean the birth of a new Mexico.

participating in the election.

As Mexico City streets surrounding the Angel of Independence filled with thousands of people, the new president's supporters broke out in a birthday song. Vicente Fox had turned 58 years old on election day.

Fox's supporters tore down a huge poster of his opponent, Francisco Labastida, that hung in the square near the Angel of Independence. "This is the moment of democracy," Fox told the crowd. "The moment of change that our country has so desired."

Starting on July 2, 2000, the election of Vicente Fox would mean that Mexico's political system would be forever changed.

In January of 2000, Vicente Fox, as the presidential candidate from the National Action Party (PAN), shows off his family's ranch. Fox spent much of his childhood at the ranch—Rancho San Cristbal, in the central Mexican state of Guanajuato—playing with the children of peasants. It was through this interaction that he first became aware of poverty.

2

A Landowner's Son Becomes Governor

Vicente Fox Quesada was the second of nine children when he was born July 2, 1942, in Mexico City. In Mexico, as in many Spanish-speaking lands, it is traditional for a baby to be given two last names. The first one, which is the last name of his father, is most commonly used. The second last name is the name of the mother's family.

Vicente Fox's mother, Mercedes Quesada, was a baby when her parents immigrated to Mexico from Spain. Fox's father, José Luis Fox, was born in Mexico but his family's roots stretch far beyond that country. José's father was an Irish immigrant who had first settled in Cincinnati, Ohio, and then moved to Mexico so that he could live in a better climate to improve his asthma. He purchased land in 1913 during the Mexican Revolution.

As a child, Fox moved to the family's San Cristbal ranch in the town of San Francisco del Rincon, which is in the central Mexican state of Guanajuato. Even though Fox's family owned a large amount of land, not all families had that privilege.

During those early childhood years, Fox began understanding the inequalities of Mexico. He spent many of his boyhood days playing with the children of peasants. Games of marbles and soccer highlighted their days, while other time was spent busying themselves by aiming slingshots at birds. Even though his grandparents were wealthy landowners, allowing Fox to lead a more privileged life, he became well aware of the poverty that surrounded him.

"I know the importance of opportunity," says Fox on his presidential website. "I grew up on the land with the children of peasants and the only thing that sets me apart from my childhood friends are the opportunities I had and they did not."

Today, a large number of poor people still live in San Cristbal, which has a population of only 2,500, along with plenty of horses and cows. The largest building in town is an old Catholic church, with 11 pews on each side, and the town's library with only two rooms. Vicente Fox's family still owns farms, canning factories and a boot company. All of these businesses employ many local residents, who say that the Fox family has been quite generous.

The state of Guanajuato, generally, is known for its charming small cities, its shoe production and for the strawberries and other produce that are grown there. But while Fox was growing up he saw many Guanajuato residents leave for the United States where they could make a better living. Eventually, the state started a program that helped Guanajuato residents who lived in the United States. It was called Casas Guanajuato.

Guanajuato and some of its neighboring states have strong ties to Catholicism, which suited Fox's family well. It is in this area of Mexico that the Cistero rebellion occurred, beginning in 1926 when Catholic militants and Mexican peasants rebelled against the ruling republican party. Vicente Fox is a strong Catholic and has always been fascinated with the Cistero rebellion. Throughout his life he has had collected books on the topic.

Vicente Fox attended Jesuit schools while growing up and even went away for his freshman year at an exclusive, private boarding school run by Jesuits in Prairie du Chien, Wisconsin. It was called Campion High School and was known for a curriculum that provided a strict education in a Catholic environment. In Wisconsin, during the school year of 1956-57, Fox became more fluent in the English language. But living in the United States and attending school in a different country was not easy for him. Vicente was a quiet student who did not fit the norm at Campion. There were 500 to 600 students at the school from at least 25 of the United States. Only a few students were from foreign countries. Classmates remembered Fox as a quiet freshman who was not yet very tall. After only one year in Wisconsin, Vicente returned in Mexico to finish high school.

In 1964 he received a degree in business administration from Universidad Iberoamericana, a Jesuit college in Mexico City. Unlike other Mexican presidents, Fox did not go away to exclusive colleges in the United States, such as Yale and Harvard. Instead, he stayed in his homeland and learned the world of business.

Immediately after graduating, Fox went to work for Coca-Cola de Mexico as a route supervisor. It was a job he has called his second university education as he traveled many of the rural routes throughout the country and learned from the people he met. During his work with Coke he learned about marketing, financial management and strategy—not in an office setting but out along the rural roads of Mexico.

In 1971 he married his first wife, Lillian de la Concha, who was his secretary at Coca-Cola. Eventually the couple adopted four children: Ana Cristina, Vicente, Paulina, and Rodrigo.

Fox's career with Coca-Cola continued to be successful. In

1975 he became chief executive of Coca-Cola in Mexico and helped the company dramatically increase soft drink sales throughout the country. Fox was among a small group of important business leaders that the president of Mexico would call in for discussions. But Vicente Fox felt that many times nothing was accomplished during those meetings.

In 1979, Coca-Cola asked Fox to oversee its operations in all of Latin America, which would have required him to move to Miami or Atlanta. He decided against it. Instead, he returned to Guanajuato where he helped several of his brothers in Grupo Fox, the family business that included the boot and shoe factories and vegetable farming.

Grupo Fox grew during that time. In 1984 the business built a new frozen food packaging plant for broccoli, cauliflower and other vegetables that was grown on the company's land. During the 1980s when Mexico was undergoing a financial crisis, several other food packagers went out of business but Grupo Fox was able to keep going.

Participating in the family business gave Fox more experience dealing with the trials of running a company. Because of his role as a director at Grupo Fox, he became a board member of the United States-Mexico Chamber of Commerce. But Fox also used other skills by participating in a variety of organizations, including several that focused on children and education. He was the founding president of the Board of Patrons of the Amigo Daniel Orphanage. And, he was President of the Loyola Board of Patrons, who are supporters the Ibero-American University of Len, and the Lux Institute, a school attended by many Guanajuato students.

In 1991 Fox and his wife separated, although he remained very active in the lives of his nearly grown children. They frequently accompanied him in his many activities.

While Fox was busy with family and volunteer activities, however, Mexico was undergoing great economic change. During the 1980s, Mexico experienced one of the greatest

This image of a Tucatecan woman in the town of Rio Lagartos, Yucatan, Mexico shows the commercial presence of Coca-Cola in the area. Much of Coca-Cola's success in Mexico was due to Fox's work as its chief executive. As the company became more influential, so did Fox.

recessions since the Great Depression. The presidencies in the country were passed from one PRI candidate to the next. In 1994 the Mexican economy experienced a banking crisis, which required help from the United States and the World Bank to stabilize businesses throughout the country.

But other changes came along that helped Mexico become more prosperous. In 1993, a major agreement was reached between Mexico, the United States and Canada. It was called the North American Free Trade Agreement (NAFTA) and it made trading with these countries easier for Mexican businesses. NAFTA also made it easier for U.S. and Canadian businesses to invest and create companies based in Mexico.

But because of NAFTA, some businesses in Mexico struggled. Others went out of businesses because it was the first time that they had strong competition. But some larger Mexican companies thrived under the NAFTA agreement. It was now easier for them to export their goods to the United States.

NAFTA caused ripples of unrest throughout Mexico. The Zapatista National Liberation Army, a group of rebels in the southern state of Chiapas, seized the city of San Cristbal de las Casas and several villages on New Year's Day in 1994. The group of rebels was made up of uneducated Tzotzil and Tzeltal Indian peasants who felt that NAFTA was a blow to their economy.

Fox never thought he would be in politics. But in the 1980s he joined the PAN party and was encouraged to become more politically active by a friend, who was one of the party leaders. Fox's friend was among several affluent Mexican business leaders who thought that the PRI's monopoly should end. Unfortunately, his friend died the following year leaving others to carry on his ideals.

As Fox continued to gain business experience, he became involved in the politics of his home state. In 1988 Fox

Former Mexican President Carlos Salinas de Gortari, shown at a news conference in Mexico City in June of 1999. Fox, as a new member of Mexico's Congress, objected immediately to the election of Salinas, who would finally leave Mexico in disgrace and become the most vilified former Mexican president in recent memory.

announced that he would run for Mexico's Congress. But soon after his announcement, some Mexican peasants illegally moved on to the Fox family's land. Vicente Fox thought they were encouraged by the PRI, which was opposed to his candidacy. Eventually, the peasants were evicted and moved away.

Fox was elected a federal deputy, or congressman, for the Third District of Len, Guanajuato, by a three-to-one vote. As a member of Mexico's Congress, he was especially interested in agricultural issues. But Fox was dismayed about the election of Carlos Salinas, the PRI candidate, to the office of Mexico's presidency. Being a new member of Congress did not stop him. Fox immediately expressed his unhappiness that Salinas' election and campaign practices were unfair.

There were hints that Fox may pursue higher political office. As early as 1993, Fox began talking about the possibility of becoming president of Mexico. The country's constitution was changed that year, enabling the children of immigrants to run for higher office as long as one parent was a native Mexican and as long as the candidate had lived in the country for at least 20 years.

Vicente Fox established an independent fund-raising organization called the Friends of Fox. But after serving two years in Congress, which meets in Mexico City, he returned to Guanajuato with thoughts of running for the position of that state's governor—a job that he knew could lead to higher office.

The first time Vicente Fox ran for the office of Guanajuato's governor, in 1991, he was not elected. His past actions came back to haunt him. Because he had expressed concern regarding Silinas' questionable election in 1988, Fox made some enemies in the PRI party. Now, there were questions surrounding Fox's loss of the governor's race. On election day more than 500 of the state's 3,850 polling stations counted more votes than there were registered voters in the district. The election commission—which was still controlled by the PRI party—certified the victory of the PRI candidate.

When citizens throughout Guanajuato's major cities protested the election's results, the PRI replaced its original candidate with a member of the PAN who they liked better than Fox. That man, however, had never been a candidate and his name had not appeared on the ballot. Fox supporters thought that he had been cheated out of the Governor's title.

In 1995, however, Fox made a comeback. During that time there was turmoil within in the PRI. An official of the PRI was assassinated and the brother of former Mexican President Carlos Salinas was arrested and later found guilty of being involved. Fox defeated his PRI opponent by a two-to-one margin.

When the new Mexican President Ernesto Zedillo had taken office in 1994 there was much work to be done. Zedillo helped the country get back on stable economic ground. Eventually, he also put widespread election reforms into place by creating the country's new Independent Electoral Commission. The commission was not affiliated with the PRI party and Mexicans hoped that it would make future elections more fair.

When elections occurred on July 6, 1997, PAN's growing importance in the country was apparent. About 26 percent of those who went to the polls, voted for a PAN candidate. The opposition party also won governships in two more states, which made of total of six states in Mexico run by governors of the PAN party.

As governor of Guanajuato, Fox worked hard and became one of Mexico's top leaders. He continuously traveled across Guanajuato and rarely spent time in his official office. He worked from his Chevrolet Suburban, from hotels and from local government offices. He spent much time working on his laptop computer writing speeches, sending e-mail, and reading Mexican newspapers online.

During Fox's administration Guanajuato became the fifth wealthiest state in the country. Fox was extremely popular both inside and outside of his home state. He frequently met with leaders of other Latin American countries and traveled to the United States to speak and meet with business consultants and governmental leaders there. He continued the Casas Guanajuato program that helped Guanajuato residents who lived in the United States. By this time, it was estimated that 4.7 million people lived in Guanajuato, but an additional 2 million of the state's official residents lived and worked in the United States.

Fox was aggressive in getting attention and more jobs for the state of Guanajuato. At a conference called the Mexico Business Peer Forum in October 1997, Fox announced that

Fox, shown here as Governor of Guanajuato in 1998. Fox worked hard as governor, crisscrossing the territory and keeping abreast of all major events, and as a result of his efforts Guanajuato became the fifth wealthiest state in Mexico. His achievement in Guanajuato turned his eyes toward the presidency.

Guanajuato would help any business build the infrastructure it needed to locate in that state. He was considered a pro-business governor by many people. He knew that bringing more businesses to Mexico would help more Mexicans get better-paying jobs.

Fox's success as governor of Guanajuato boosted his ambitions of seeking the presidency. Others in Mexico were also well aware that Fox had higher political aspirations and they did not necessarily like that. His opponents in the PRI party sometimes expressed their displeasure. But Fox was not about to quit. Before his term as Guanajuato's governor was up, Vicente Fox had declared his desire to be president of Mexico.

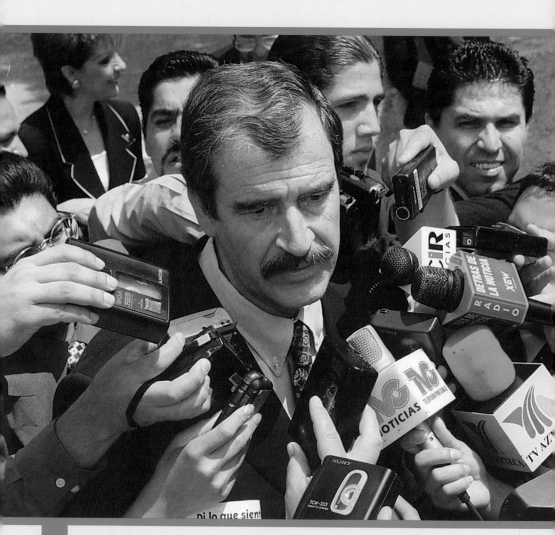

Before his presidential candidacy for the National Action Party (PAN), Vicente Fox speaks with reporters on in May of 1999 in Mexico City. Fox began his campaign in 1997 with only the support of the Friends of Fox, and he was named as the PAN's candidate late in 1999.

3

A Presidential Campaign

V icente Fox was greeted with a booming brass band and thousands of Mayan farmers who were gathered in the colonial plaza of the city of Valladolid. It was a hot weekend in May 1998, and the end of a whirlwind tour Fox had taken in his Chevrolet Suburban. He had visited several towns on the Yucatan Peninsula, which is located on the east coast of Mexico, to talk about his campaign for president. Fox believed that many Mexicans were ready to vote against the PRI.

Vicente Fox announced that he was candidate for Mexico's president near the end of 1997. Instead of waiting around for PAN's support, he quickly started his campaign by establishing the Friends of Fox, an organization that collected contributions from supporters. Many of Fox's main supporters, however, did not want to be named because they feared reprisal by the PRI, whose members had ruled the country for more than years.

For decades there had been wide corruption among Mexican businesses and political leaders. The PRI was blamed for murders, massacres and crime throughout that time. Many businesses were profitable because their leaders had good relationships with people who ran the PRI. The government approved laws that benefited certain companies, which made the company owners very wealthy. Yet, the wages for Mexico's workers were rarely increased, leaving many Mexican peasants extremely poor.

In the past, Mexico's wealthiest business owners had supported the PRI. But during Fox's campaign, the country's wealthy businessmen were less vocal about their favorite presidential candidate. They said they were neutral, even though many people started suspecting that they supported Fox. Unlike the United States where laws require that political contributors be named in public, Mexico had no such requirements. All of this mystery even added more intrigue to the campaign.

The cozy relationship between some business owners and government officials stagnated in the 1980s when some business owners entered politics. A man named Ernesto Ruffo, an executive for a fishing company in the state of Baja California, became the first governor of a Mexican state who was from an opposition party. He was elected in 1989 and represented the PAN party. Without men like Ruffo paving the way, Vicente Fox's campaign for president may have never occurred.

Fox's candidacy for the country's top position changed the way that Mexican politics had been run for more than seven decades. No longer would Mexico's top official be chosen from nominations of only the PRI. The election of 2000 would be different.

Vicente Fox was known as the very eager, early bird candidate, because he started campaigning three years before the election. But there were other opposition candidates interested in the presidency, too. Fox knew he needed to work hard to get to know people throughout Mexico. When it was time for

A carrier truck leaves the General Motors assembly plant in Silao, a major employer of residents of Guanajuato, in March of 1996. Fox sought to increase American business interest in Guanajuato in order to create more jobs.

Election Day in 2000, he wanted to be the candidate foremost in the voters' minds.

During the spring of 1998 Fox was traveled across Mexico and in the United States talking about his platform for the presidency. Many Mexicans who live and work in the United States still have the ability to vote in their home country because they retain their residency status there. Fox traveled so much one band wrote a song about him called "Traveling Boots."

While visiting Philadelphia, Fox opened a Guanajuato office in that city to help his state attract businesses from the United States. General Motors already had a manufacturing plant in the Guanajuato town of Silao. Fox wanted more jobs available to local residents like those provided by General Motors.

Fox did other things while he visited the United States, too. He talked with a Nobel Prize-winning economist and some other consultants in Philadelphia. Then he traveled to Dallas where he planned to open a warehouse called the Guanajuato Trading Outlet, which would help Guanajuato entrepreneurs more easily trade with Texas business owners. He stayed busy making contacts throughout two countries that would benefit him if he became president.

Thanks to Fox, the campaign for Mexico's presidential election of 2000 started early. Candidates who were only contemplating the race were pushed into campaigning once Fox had announced his candidacy. Cuauhtémoc Cárdenas, the mayor of Mexico City, was among other opposition candidates seeking the position. Cardenas, the son of a former Mexican president, was a member of the Democratic Revolutionary Party, known as the PRD. Several PRI officials wanted the office, too.

Frequently, Fox talked about his surprise at finding himself in politics. He often recalled that his father said that only thieves and crooks entered politics in Mexico. But it was Fox's enthusiasm for removing the PRI from Mexico's top office that propelled him forward. His service in Mexico's Congress and his work as Guanajuato's governor had convinced him that he was capable of helping Mexico. Even his failed 1991 race for governor, which he believed was marked by fraud, helped to convince him that he could make Mexico a better place to live.

Fox continued to travel throughout the country. He visited Mexico City's central wholesale market to shake hands with vegetable vendors and others at the open-air market. It was still two years before the presidential election and many of the people there had not yet heard about Fox. It would take nearly all of that time for Vicente Fox to be a recognized name among the many Mexicans who would go to the voting polls. When he visited the Mexican market it seemed that Mexicans liked him. His tall stature drew their attention, but his jeans and cowboy boots made them feel comfortable. Fox dressed like the working men and women throughout Mexico. Many vendors felt that they could talk to Fox and that he was interested in their opinions because he was also a farmer.

Throughout his campaign Fox talked about the plans he had for Mexico. Fox discussed his poor agricultural home state of Guanajuato, where thousands of people left every year to find work in the United States. But Fox also pointed out that during his term as governor Guanajuato became more prosperous. He emphasized the fact that all of Mexico needed more businesses, like those that he was able to lure to Guanajuato. New businesses meant more jobs and that was one of Fox's top campaign promises.

Fox also talked about Guanajuato's new scholarship system that guaranteed education through the university level for any child who worked hard in school. Fox wanted to double the amount of money that Mexico spent on education to ensure that all Mexicans had access to free schools.

Fox also discussed a new micro loan program that offered small business loans to entrepreneurs in the state. In 1997, 35,000 people in Guanajuato received micro loans. Many of them were women who purchased sewing machines or tamale-making machines so that they could sell their creations. The micro loan program was one of the governor's ways of encouraging the state's residents to make more money.

In addition, Fox talked about the new initiatives in Guanajuato that helped fight corruption. Education and training requirements were put into place for the police. Judges' salaries were dramatically increased so they would be less susceptible to taking bribes.

Fox thought that the same basic goals that he had in Guanajuato could be carried out throughout the country. His top goal, always, was to take the presidential seat away from the members of the PRI party that he felt had been unjust to Mexico's people during its reign.

Fox also pledged to the Mexican people that he would help

the country by making Mexico a wealthier government. He wanted to see a seven percent growth in the economy by the second half of his six-year term. Also, he promised to improve Mexico's method of collecting taxes. Mexico's taxes are much lower than taxes in the United States. Under Fox's plan, more taxes would be collected to help the country's schools, roads and public hospitals.

Fox talked about giving more money to help small farmers. He said he would modernize Petroleos Mexicanos, also called Pemex, the Mexico-owned oil company. He also wanted to give raises to thousands of Pemex employees.

Fox also promised to cooperate with the United States in its fight against illegal drugs. During the 1990s the United States government estimated that about 80 percent of the cocaine entering the U.S. either originated in or passed through Mexico. It also estimated that Mexican drug lords were making $10 to $30 billion dollars a year. Fox knew it would be difficult to have a good relationship with the United States if his country remained responsible for the huge drug trade.

Plus, Fox wanted to start peace talks with the Zapatista rebels rebelled in the southern Mexican state of Chiapas in 1994. These rebels were mainly Indians who accused the Mexican government of 500 years of exploitation. If elected president, Fox wanted to preside over a peaceful country.

Because of his experience with being a governor, Fox thought that states needed to have more power to rule their own affairs. He proposed that states in Mexico develop more autonomy.

Fox had other concerns, too. He was bothered by the fact that Mexicans could earned as little as $5 a day, but if they crossed the border into the United States they could earn $60 to $80 a day. As long as Mexicans weren't valued in their own country, he knew that they would flee to look for jobs elsewhere.

In the early days of his campaign, Fox also talked about establishing a currency board that would fix the value of the peso to the United States' or another country's dollar. A currency

A ship passes near part of an oil platform of Mexico's state oil company, Petroleos Mexicanos (Pemex), in Campeche in August of 2001. Fox wanted to modernize Pemex and to increase the wages of its employees.

board would make sure that every Mexican peso that is in circulation would be backed by an American dollar, or currency from another country that was owned by the Mexican government. This is a way that the Mexican government could provide more stability to the value of the peso. During his early campaign, Fox also mentioned that in twenty or thirty years there should be a common currency between Mexico, Canada and the United States—a dollar or coins that would be valued at the same amount in all three countries. Later, he seemed to forget about that idea.

While Fox continued to campaign, PRI officials appeared to be growing nervous. In the summer of 1998 a group of PRI Congressmen proposed a new law that would return to the system that prohibited citizens with a foreign-born parent from running for president. The proposal was aimed directly at Vicente Fox. But the proposal never passed in Congress. Fox seemed undaunted. By the end of the summer he was in Oakland, California, assuring a gathering of a local organization that he would be the next president of Mexico.

Fox worked hard during the next several months continuing to travel and talk to the people of Mexico. Often his 19-year-old daughter, Ana Cristina, accompanied him. He still needed much more support to win the presidency. Even some people in his own PAN party did not support him. Many of those who did not support Fox were descendants of Catholic politicians who had founded the PAN party in 1938. They wanted to continue with the party's original religious, conservative doctrine. Fox knew that an ultra-conservative PAN candidate would never become Mexico's president.

In the spring of 1999 PAN elected a new party president, Luis Felipe Bravo Mena, who was more supportive of Fox's campaign. The new party president aimed to help unite members of the PAN party.

In addition to the PAN, there were other opposition groups such as the PRD. One idea that several politicians discussed was uniting all opposition parties in Mexico to find one candidate who could oppose the PRI candidate. Some thought this was the only way that they could keep the PRI candidate out of the president's office.

But Fox didn't agree that all opposition parties should support one candidate. His views on several issues were very different from other candidates. For example, the PRD's Cuauhtémoc Cárdenas talked about renegotiating NAFTA with the United States and Canada. Fox supported the agreement in its current form. Also, Fox thought that Mexico's petroleum industry should be owned by private companies, but Cardenas' father had created the government-owned Pemex when he was president.

Some of Fox's supporters liked the fact that he was a businessman before he became a politician. They thought he understood what it were like to be both a big business executive and a small business owner because he had worked for the gigantic Coca-Cola and for his family's smaller company. In Mexico, NAFTA's approval divided the largest businesses from the smaller ones. Large businesses, especially those that created goods for exports, seemed to profit under NAFTA while smaller businesses suffered when more foreign competitors entered the country. During his campaign, Fox thought he could pull together both sets of business owners.

Even though Fox felt like some Mexican companies were corrupt and that they had become wealthy by doing illegal things, he was adamant that he would not waste time by punishing those who broke laws in the past. Fox talked often about looking forward, toward Mexico's future, instead of looking back and placing blame for past problems in Mexico.

Mexico's 2000 presidential campaign was making a lot of history. In addition to Fox announcing his candidacy years in advance of the election, television also played an important role. For the first time in Mexico's history all of its presidential candidates began running television commercials. This allowed some people in even the most remote areas of the country to see and hear from their presidential candidates.

In 1994, only the PRI had used television to promote its candidate. Opposition candidates could not get on the PRI-controlled airwaves. But in the election of 2000, all presidential candidates were provided with some government funding to purchase television air time.

Being on television was an advantage for the handsome Vicente Fox. As a businessman, he knew he would need help portraying the correct image for the campaign. He hired a

Mexico City, April 25, 2000: Supporters of Institutional Revolutionary Party candidate Francisco Labastida, Fox's major opponent in the 2000 election, watch as Fox speaks on national television. This was the first presidential debate ever to be held in Mexico.

former Procter & Gamble marketing specialist to direct his broadcast campaign and he consulted with political advisor Dick Morris, who had worked with United States President Bill Clinton.

Fox's six-and-a-half foot stature, in some way, helped add to his presidential appearance. In advertisements, he was portrayed as a businessman who could bring foreign investors to Mexico and he was shown as a strong family man who was concerned about Mexico's poor people. His worst moment on television came during a political debate between him and his two opponents. Fox appeared to be stubborn as he presented his side of the discussion.

Nonetheless, after nearly two years Fox's television advertisements made him one of the most recognizable candidates in the field. But running television advertisements was expensive and Fox's funds for advertising dwindled as the campaign continued.

Another popular television candidate was the PRI's Roberto Madrazo, a former governor of another Mexican state. Madrazo contracted with the son of a notable Mexican film director who had also produced advertising for Ernesto Zedillo's campaign in 1994.

Eventually, many of the Mexican presidential candidates began seeking advice from media consultants in the United States. Another favorite PRI candidate, Francisco Labastida, interviewed several media advisors including James Carville, who led President Bill Clinton's campaign in the United States in 1992. In the end, Labastida employed a Mexican firm to create his advertising campaign.

Because of his dwindling campaign account, in the latter days of 1999 Fox was forced to figure out a way that got him back on the air waves. During President Zedillo's annual state of the union address to Congress in 1999, Fox walked on to the Congressional floor—even though only elected officials were allowed to be there. He stopped to shake hands and pat the back of PAN congressmen, and then he left the room halfway through Zedillo's speech. Afterward, he told reporters that the stunt was the only way he could get on television.

Evidently, Fox's appearance didn't detract from his popularity. Less than two weeks later he was officially nominated the PAN's presidential candidate. Even though he was unopposed in the PAN's primary election, it was the first time a primary vote of that political party was held in public. Previous elections had forced PAN business to be conducted in closed conventions out of fear of reprisal from the ruling PRI party.

Still, Fox was disappointed to find that he was favored by only slightly more than one-third of registered PAN voters. Others voted for him, too, though. Mexicans who were not PAN members were able to vote for Fox by writing his name on informal ballots.

Fox's campaign got more attention when the candidate made a faux pas later that week. As he spoke at a campaign rally in Guanajuato, two of his children presented a pennant to him that had the image of the Virgin of Guadalupe, a Mexican-Catholic enigma. Fox said that the Virgin was an inspiration to him.

However, some Mexicans disagreed with Fox's actions saying that politics should not include references to the church. Most Mexicans believe that the church and state need to be kept separate due to the country's bloody past. Although Fox didn't appear to break any rules by holding the banner, both the Mexican constitution and Mexican laws prohibit the use of religious emblems from being used in the names of political parties or in political campaigns. Evidently, Fox thought his actions could help him get support from PAN members, many of whom were devout Catholics who honored the Virgin of Guadalupe.

It wasn't long until Oct. 10, when the PRD, the other major opposition party, officially nominated its presidential contender. Again there was only one candidate. Mexico City Mayor Cuauhtemoc Cardenas received the nomination.

As the November 7 date for the PRI primary election drew closer, Fox and his supporters revisited the idea of joining forces with the PRD for an opposition primary. By this time, Fox had garnered much more support than Cardenas. However, Fox still did not have the full support of the PAN. None of the party's leadership called him after he gave his acceptance speech following the primary. After weeks of discussion, the opposition primary fizzled out because Fox and PAN leaders feared that there would be fraud to get the PRD candidate elected.

On November 7 the PRI elected Labastida as its candidate for president. Now the real race would begin. The campaign of 2000 was a tense time, a time when at least one of the opposition candidates would truly challenge the ruling PRI party. Mexico braced for another election that many feared would take a turn to violence. Labastida beat out two other PRI candidates, the good-looking Tabasco governor Roberto Madrazo and former interior minister Manuel Bartlett.

With his opponents now identified, Fox spent months crossing through Mexico in his bright blue campaign bus. Painted on the bus's side was his slogan: "Change has arrived."

On a warm spring night, the weary candidate was met by 8,000 people as he spoke in Sinaloa, Labastida's home state. Fistfights broke out but Fox continued to flash his V-for-victory sign with two of his fingers. He would not give up. Despite the dangers it might entail, Vicente Fox's main goal was to replace the PRI in the office of Mexico's president.

He diffused some of the angry crowd by talking with those who were bitter about past elections. Then he ripped into a riveting speech lambasting the culture of violence and drugs for which Sinaloa is known.

Fox campaigned tirelessly. He visited the city of Saltillo, in northeast Mexico, and talked to 3,000 university students about democracy—a foreign concept to many who lived there. Later, at a luncheon with business leaders, he promised to create 1.3 million new jobs each year and talked about forming a free market for trade.

Fox targeted specific Mexican groups in order to get more votes. He appealed to women, who rarely voted, to participate in the election. He also tried to convince college students of the importance of their votes.

Even though Fox had closely trailed Labastida in the polls

Fox speaks at a campaign rally in Queretaro, Mexico in June of 2000. At this point, Fox and Labastida were in a dead heat in the polls, and the possibility of the PRI's defeat attracted international attention.

that try to predict who would win the election, by the end of May the two candidates were in a dead heat. Political leaders in the United States and other countries began looking at the Mexican race very carefully, surprised that the PRI candidate was being seriously challenged.

"When is Mexico going to change?" Fox called out to the thousands of people who gathered to hear him speak days before election day in the town of Minatitlan, located on Mexico's Gulf Coast.

"Today," the crowd shouted back at him.

When he visited another nearby town, Fox climbed on a big, green John Deere tractor and, holding his straw hat to his head, began to drive around. Fox raised his other hand to show his traditional V sign. The crowd roared.

Still, not everyone in Mexico agreed that Fox should be the next president. Many voters did not like his stand against abortion. He made statements that opposed homosexuals. Some did not agree with him that schools should teach religious values and others feared that he would attempt to inflict his personal, strict Catholic viewpoint, on the country of Mexico.

In the waning days of the campaign, Fox tried to appeal to some of these concerns. He made a commitment for public education. He said he would limit the power of the presidency. And he promised that he would fight poverty in favor of equality.

Enough voters believed him. On July 2, 2000, Vicente Fox got the best birthday present of his life. He made Mexican history by defeating the PRI candidate and winning the country's presidency.

As President-elect, Vicente Fox prepares to tape a television program at Rancho San Cristbal in Guanajuato on November 25, 2000. Fox was inaugurated as Mexico's first opposition president a week later, on December 1.

4

Five Long Months: A Transition

V icente Fox was filled with pride and love for his Mexican countrymen when he was pronounced the winner of the presidential elections. "I have never been so in love with my country, and with each and every one of you," he told the thousands of supporters who gathered at the Angel of Independence in Mexico City.

But later that night, Mexicans who were at the Angel of Independence started a chant that reflected the thoughts of Mexicans across the country. "Don't fail us," they shouted. "Don't fail us."

The pressure was on. Fox knew he had much work to do before he would move into Los Pinos, the Mexican presidential residence, on December 1. He would need to select members of his cabinet, he would need to continue communications with the people of Mexico, and he would need to reorganize Mexico's government. It would be a government that was not ruled by the PRI and one that was independent, not dependant on the PAN or any other political party. It would be busy five months before Vicente Fox would be inaugurated as Mexico's president.

Newspapers from Mexico City to Los Angeles to New York said that Foxmania had swept over Mexico. Even Mexicans who voted for Fox appeared stunned that the candidate had won over Labistida, the PRI party's candidate. Fox's hard work traveling around the country had paid off. The election results showed that he won in every region of Mexico, but he was most popular in the northern segment of the country.

In the hours after he was elected, Fox didn't waste any time. He gave victory speeches to the public and on Mexico's national television, he had a short toast to his victory, and then he buckled down to work.

Fox was extremely aware that his election had ended more than 70 years of what had been nearly a Mexican dictatorship and he was careful with his expectations. He knew that he had to maintain the support of the Mexicans who had voted him into office, but he also knew that he would need money and time before his ideas could be put to work for Mexico.

It was rare for Mexicans to experience a peaceful election when the ruling party was being challenged. But Fox was aware that most victories by opposition candidates had caused upheaval across the country. Throughout his campaign he attempted to convince Mexicans that change would be good. In the aftermath of his victory he emphasized the need for unity, even extending a welcoming gesture to his rival candidates.

Fox had made new friends during his campaign. He had visited with farmers in the rural southern territory of the country and factory employees in the north. Even Mexico's intellectuals, college professors and the like, decided that Fox was their best candidate. In the end Fox, the farmer and businessman, seemed to have been all of Mexico's favorite candidate.

In addition to Fox's election, PAN's political party celebrated much success. The party had the biggest number of people

Fox, right, and outgoing President Ernesto Zedillo meet at the presidential residence, Los Pinos, in Mexico City in November of 2000, just before Fox's inauguration. Zedillo was the last of 71 years of presidents from the PRI. Largely through his creation of the Federal Electoral Institute, Zedillo had completely reformed the Mexican system of elections. The election of 2000 enabled Mexico to be perceived as a democracy by the world community.

elected to Mexico's Senate. Now more members of PAN had seats in both segments of Mexico's Congress—the Chamber of Representatives and the Chamber of the Senate. Even though PAN did not have a majority of members in either segment of Congress, the party had more members than any of Mexico's political parties, including the PRI.

President Ernesto Zedillo promised Fox that he would work hard with him to provide an efficient handover of the government in December. This was not an easy task since the PRI had ruled Mexico for so long. Even though there had been many elections in Mexico's past, the one of July 2000 marked the first time that Mexico was looked at by the rest of the world as having a democracy in place. Zedillo was credited with reforming Mexico's election system by creating the independent Federal Electoral Institute. Former United States President Jimmy Carter and others monitored the presidential election in 2000 to be sure that there was no fraud.

Zedillo's reforms had also provided Fox and the other candidates with $1 billion that was used for their broadcast advertising time. Zedillo took great pride in the election procedure. Many people thought that without his reformation of the election system, Fox could not have been elected president.

Fox considered it a great challenge to oversee a peaceful transition of the government. In the days that followed the election, Zedillo also used his power to help the transition be smoothly done. He met with the 21 Mexican governors who were members of the PRI and encouraged them to help create a peaceful transition of the presidency.

"Today we have shown for all to see that ours is a nation of free men and women who believe in the means of democracy and law to achieve progress," Zedillo told television viewers in his address on election night.

Not everyone was happy, though. Many members of the PRI blamed Zedillo for the party's loss of the presidency. In the aftermath of losing the election, Mexicans even wondered if the PRI would survive as a political party. Some voters said that the PRI was out of touch with the younger voters who were 18 to 35 years old. Those voters agreed with Fox that education and jobs needed to be a priority for the country. Many of them lived in the highly industrialized areas in north Mexico. PRI leaders found that their supporters during the election lived in the poorer, more rural southern states. Even PRI leaders could not agree with each other on how the party should go about getting new voters.

Statesmen around the world recognized that political power was changing in Mexico and different countries evaluated how Mexico's change would affect them. Bill Clinton, who was the United States' president at the time that Fox was elected to power, immediately called him with congratulations. In the United States, Clinton released a statement congratulating all of Mexico. "Mexicans should be proud of the extraordinary steps they have taken during the last six years to strengthen and consolidate democratic institutions and set Mexico on a course of economic growth and prosperity," Clinton said.

The three main issues that concerned the United States and Mexico were immigration, the import and export of products, and the flow of illegal drugs across the border. Zedillo had created good relations with the United States during his six years in office and Clinton and other officials wanted to be sure that progress would be made during Fox's term in office.

Fox had much work to do in the months before he took office. Sunday night, after the election, he only slept five hours. Monday evening he met with Zedillo and the two of them set about the work of the transition, even agreeing that they would create Mexico's budget for the upcoming year together. Administrators at the Mexico Interior Ministry began talking to Fox about plans for his personal security.

During the first week after Election Day, Fox knew it was important to stay in touch with Mexicans. He gave several interviews to newspaper reporters from Mexico and the United States, held a two-hour press conference and appeared on several television call-in talk shows. Following Mexico's first truly democratic election, Fox knew he was accountable to the people who put him in office.

He quickly established plans for the following months. He planned to meet with all of the governors of Mexico's 31 states and he planned to travel to other Latin American countries, the United States, and Europe. Fox also announced that he would seek three contenders to interview for each position in his presidential cabinet before he would choose a person to fill each of those spots. But he gave himself only two months to fill his cabinet positions.

Fox contacted several international headhunting firms to help him seek the Mexico's most qualified candidates for his cabinet. He promised that even candidates who supported the PRI and the PDR would be considered for the jobs. Fox's record as Guanajuato's governor attested to his openness to include other parties. A member of the PRI had been his finance secretary.

Fox was already working with a small group of advisers that included a former executive of the World Bank, a former communist, and a team of three administrators who had worked in his Guanajuato government. Fox tackled the President's job as though he were organizing a big company. He promised his constituents that he would balance Mexico's budget and that he would be careful about the money that the government spent. Because Fox had increased Coca-Cola sales in Mexico by 32 percent during the time he was president of the organization, many people had great expectations for Fox.

Mexico's new president also immediately began preparing a six-year plan for his presidency that he would announce at his December 1 inauguration. But he was also looking at Mexico's future beyond those six years. He requested that intellectuals at Mexico's universities and think tanks prepare a long-term, 25-year vision for the country. Fox wanted a blueprint that would guide Mexico into becoming a more prosperous country and one that focused on human rights.

Some worried that none of Fox's changes would go into effect. Millions of Mexicans who worked for that country's federal government could block some changes. PRI governors in the majority of the Mexican states could ignore other changes. Also, the Mexican Congress could defeat some of Fox's proposals since his PAN party did not hold a majority vote. Certainly, change for Mexico was not going to be easy.

At a colonial museum in the historic district of the Mexico City, Fox introduces eight members of his Cabinet to the media on November 22, 2000. Applying his business acumen to the presidency, Fox had considered candidates from multiple parties and had employed a headhunting agency to find them.

But there was no time to be wasted. Fox knew that the people of Mexico had voted for him because they expected change and he knew that he must quickly act. As one of his first orders of business, he announced that he would strip the Interior Ministry of its police and security powers and that he would take power away from the attorney general's office. At the time, he attorney general's office was responsible for investigating drug trafficking but many people believed that there was corruption in that office. Fox planned to create a Ministry of Security and Justice that would oversee the federal police and the court system. The interior ministry had been accused of spying on Mexican residents, of rigging elections, and of covering up killings that were committed by police officers.

Fox saw Mexico's corruption as one of his biggest challenges. He wanted to create an openness among police, security agents, and others. He talked of forming a truth commission that would investigate corruption. Even though Fox invited most employees of the federal government to keep their jobs, he insisted that there would need to be a change in attitude with more accountability and honesty.

Fox continued to work on his goal of reducing poverty in Mexico by bringing more jobs into the country and by making more loans available to Mexicans. Another long-term goal was to get the United States and Canada to legalize Mexican workers, so that these people were not considered illegal aliens. He wanted more Mexicans to be given the status of guest worker that was already given to some Mexicans working in the United States. But, he also knew that fewer Mexicans would need to work in the United States if there were more and better paying jobs in Mexico.

Throughout the summer, various issues competed for Fox's attention. By August he had made several appointments to his cabinet. Luis Derbez, an economist who was educated in the United States, was put in charge of the economic transition team.

During the months before he took the presidency, Fox tried repeatedly to communicate with the Zapatista rebels in the state of Chiapas. There was an eerie silence from the group and his requests went unanswered. The Zapatistas had been rebelling against the Mexican government since New Years Day in 1994 when the rebels seized San Cristbal de las Casas and several other villages throughout Chiapas. At least 100 people had died when the Mexican armed forces entered the area after the initial uprising. The rebels had disappeared into the jungle where they stayed for most of the last six years.

During the campaign Fox had announced his desire to increase trade between Mexico and South American countries. In the late summer, he visited Brazil, Ecuador, Uruguay, and other countries in an effort to work toward trade agreements.

After that he focused on relations with Canada and the United States. While in Canada for two days he advocated a more open border policy, then he traveled to the United States he met with President Clinton and others. While he was giving a speech to the National Press Club in Washington, Fox suggested that the United States should spend less money on guarding the Mexican border and more money on helping businesses invest in Mexico.

He also met with Vice President Al Gore and Texas Governor George W. Bush, both of whom were candidates for the United States presidency in November 2000. Fox talked about his goals to open the NAFTA agreement to create more open borders and labor markets. A sticky issue had arisen since NAFTA went into effect in 1994. Despite the agreement, President Clinton had forbidden Mexican trucks from crossing the border into the United States. Clinton said it was because of safety concerns.

In Washington, Fox also met with environmentalists and human rights leaders. Environmentalists were concerned with issues such as the protection of sea turtles and dolphins that roam both United States and Mexican waters. Human rights leaders had voiced ongoing concerns regarding corruption and poverty in Mexico.

Fox's work did not stop there. In October, he traveled to Brussels and other European countries to discuss issues that affected Mexico.

Fox wanted to make big changes for Mexicans, but people in that country were impatient. By October when Fox's advisor on economic matters announced that the new President's goal of a seven percent economic growth would probably not occur until 2004, Mexicans took offense. They were not willing to put Fox's promises on hold for a few years; they wanted immediate action. Although he had not even taken office, the new president knew that he must act quickly, or he would be immediately criticized.

Fox and U.S. President Bill Clinton joke in the Rose Garden of the White House on August 24, 2000, during Fox's two-day visit. As he had done in Canada, Fox lobbied for open borders and encouraged foreign investment in Mexico. Clinton called Fox's election a "truly historic affirmation of democracy" in Mexico.

In November Fox traveled to California to establish working relations with officials of the state that purchased more Mexican goods and services than any other in the United States.

During all the planning for his presidential duties, Fox had to find the time to plan his inauguration. It would be a huge celebration featuring three days with events in four different cities. By the time December 1 came, the whole world would be watching Vicente Fox become president of Mexico.

Making his characteristic V-for-victory sign, Fox celebrates his inauguration day in Mexico City on December 1, 2000 with a group of street children. Most Mexicans had always lived under single-party rule.

5

Keeping Promises

Many Mexicans wept tears of joy on December 1, 2000, when Vicente Fox was inaugurated into the office of Mexico's presidency. Many Mexicans were happy that change was occurring for their government and they had high hopes that Fox could improve their lives and the lives of their children.

Mexicans gathered in public squares in Mexico City to cheer on their new president during the inaugural ceremonies. In rural areas and smaller cities, people gathered around televisions to watch the proceedings. Most Mexicans had only lived during the time that PRI officials ruled the country. Few could believe that the PRI candidate was not being inaugurated into the office of the president.

It was Friday, the beginning of a busy weekend for Vicente Fox. The morning of Fox's inauguration started as he went to pray at the Basilica de Guadalupe, a shrine to Mexico's patron saint. His youngest daughter, Paulina, presented him with a crucifix while he was at the podium there. He then had breakfast with hundreds of homeless children, mental health patients, and street vendors in the small community of Tepito.

Fox would be a different kind of president for Mexico. By having breakfast with this group of people he was making a silent statement that he was concerned with all of Mexico's population, not only the privileged class of businessmen who had greatly benefited with their ties to the PRI and past presidents of the country.

Fox's inauguration day was one of the most important days of his life. He was dressed in a dark suit with shiny cufflinks on his shirtsleeves and a formal tie around his neck. He even had a special pair of boots made from ostrich and goat leather for the event.

Fox was sworn in by Mexico's Congress. President Zedillo presented him with a satiny sash in Mexico's colors of red, green, and white that he slipped around his neck. He began his formal speech by greeting each of his four children by name. Then Mexico's new president talked about the country's past reformers, many of whom were killed as they led their crusades. He then promised that he would live up to his ideals to reform Mexico and he spoke of plans for his new government.

Fox's address was briefly interrupted when some PRI members of Congress shouted out in the crowd to heckle the country's new leader. Fox took their shouts in stride. Smiling, he asked them to calm down and eventually they did.

Fox followed his speech to Congress with another talk at the National Auditorium that was filled with his supporters. "To all Mexicans I say, 'We have a date with history. We are up to the task,'" he said to those in the auditorium and to Mexicans throughout the country who were watching on television. "I seek no greater privilege than to serve all of you, serve your children and serve all of Mexico."

Fox assured his countrymen that he would uphold his

campaign promises. He planned to lift Mexicans out of poverty and rid the country of the corruption that was ruining it.

Fox's new cabinet members were inaugurated on television as Fox read the government ethics rules, which prohibit cabinet members from taking money from anyone who would compromise their ability to make unbiased decisions. His cabinet members swore that they would uphold those rules.

Fox installed one of the largest cabinets that Mexico had seen in years. It included 50 cabinet and sub-cabinet members who would give the president advice. They came from different political parties and different backgrounds. Fox's treasury secretary, Francisco Gil, had worked for an earlier PRI president, Carlos Salinas. Gil, who was educated as an economist at the University of Chicago in the United States, had the reputation of making sure that all of Mexico's taxes were collected.

One of Fox's long-time advisors throughout his campaign, Jorge Castaneda, became his new foreign secretary. Castaneda's father had held the same position under a PRI president, but the younger Castaneda was an outspoken opponent of the PRI. Fox employed a woman as his spokesman. Martha Sahagun had worked with him since his first campaign for the Guanajuato governor's office.

Fox looked to another former corporate leader to oversee the state's oil monopoly, Pemex. He asked Raul Munoz, a former Dupont executive in Mexico, to oversee the management and finances of the state-owned company. Energy issues would take an important place in the new government.

As darkness began to fall on the night of Fox's inauguration, Mexico's new President stood on the balcony of the National Palace and led thousands of Mexicans in a patriotic rally. After he was finished, he took off his suit jacket and went into the plaza, where he sat on a stage with other people. An 18th century castle in nearby Chapultepec Park was the site for his formal inaugural dinner later that evening.

Fox's presidency was already having an effect on Mexico. Just two days before Fox took office, the leader of the Zapatista National Liberation Army issued a terse statement wishing Zedillo farewell.

The day after Fox was inaugurated, the leader, known as Subcommander Marcos, spoke at a news conference called at his jungle headquarters. Marcos wore a black wool ski mask over his face to protect his identity and held a high-powered rifle on his lap as he announced that his group wanted to restart negotiations for peace in the state of Chiapas.

Marcos said the Zapatistas had several issues they wanted addressed. They wanted the government to remove troops from their territory and they wanted all Zapatistas released from prison. There were other requests, too.

Fox was ready to begin negotiations. Even before the requests were made by the Zapatistas, the evening of his inauguration he had ordered troops to start moving out of Chiapas. He said he would focus on the rebels' other requests in days to come. The situation in Chiapas would be a proving ground for Fox's ability to pull together the Mexican people. The Zapatista rebels said that they planned to send 24 of their leaders to Mexico City in February to discuss their plight with Congress.

Much was going on in the administration of President Fox by his second day in office. The morning was spent visiting some of the military and in the afternoon Fox met with the leaders of Mexico's indigenous communities that lived in poverty. In the southern city of Oaxaca he was greeted by nearly 10,000 teachers, farmers, and workers who begged him for justice. Fox promised that national funding would become available to help them improve education and to lower prices for cooking gas. Still, many of these people refused to believe his promises. It would be difficult for Fox to convince the poor people living in the southern Mexican states that he was on their side.

Throughout the next two months Fox worked hard on his agenda. In mid-February he met with United States

In a highly unusual public display of force, Zapatista rebel leader Sub-commandante Marcos, on horseback at left, leads his troops into the meeting ground at the Zapatista headquarters in La Realidad, Chiapas, in 1995. In 2000, the Zapatistas wanted to negotiate for peace in the state of Chiapas, and President Fox began to address their demands even on his first day in office.

Congressman Luis V. Gutierrez who had introduced legislation into the U.S. Congress that would legalize illegal Mexican immigrants who did not have the appropriate paperwork to live in the United States.

Later that same week, the two countries' national anthems

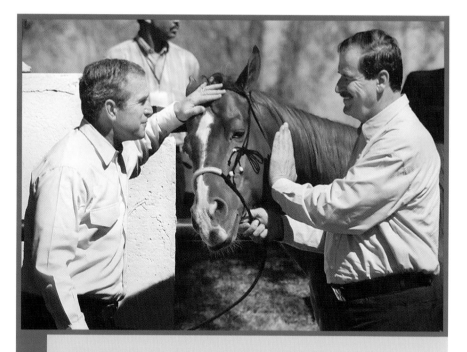

President Fox and U.S. President George W. Bush pet a horse at Rancho San Cristbal, about 210 miles northwest of Mexico City, on February 16, 2001. On the agenda for discussion during the newly elected President Bush's visit were issues of border and immigration policy, trade, education, and crime–in particular the drug trade.

played as newly-elected United States President George W. Bush arrived in Mexico. Bush and Fox planned to discuss immigration and other issues. The two men had already met when each were governors—Bush of Texas and Fox of Guanajuato. But this meeting would hold more importance. Both men were now presidents of their countries.

Fox thought it was important that he and Bush meet in Guanajuato, his home state. As their cars headed toward Fox's ranch, they passed clusters of goats grazing in fields and signs that bore flags of both nations. The two presidents stopped for a short visit with Fox's mother and, later, the mayor of San Cristbal presented Bush with a pair of shiny black cowboy boots. Eventually, they settled in for discussions at Fox's small home which sat next to a field of broccoli.

Mexico's vast supply of oil was on Bush's mind. California was experiencing a power crisis and Bush knew that Mexico's ability to produce and export electricity and natural gas could be helpful. Border policies and immigration, of course, were important issues for Fox. The two men also discussed trade between the two nations, the expansion of educational opportunities, and their concerns regarding crime and the illegal drug trafficking.

Of course, both men knew that it would take months, maybe even years, before progress would be made on any of their issues. This first meeting of the two presidents was symbolic. Many people thought it was the first time that an American president had gone out of his way soon after taking office to make Mexico feel as though it was an important neighbor. President Bush wanted to establish a strong bond with the United States' southern neighbor and this visit was only the beginning of that process. At the end of a long afternoon of discussions, the two presidents made joint statements.

"Mr. President Bush, the spirit in which we have conducted this first working meeting marks the beginning of a novel stage in our bilateral relations," said Fox. "I am certain that we will be able to take advantage of the historic opportunity we have today to set out on the way to a century of shared prosperity. We will face this challenge on the basis of mutual trust, with a fresh and creative vision to advance in the topics of our bilateral agenda. Once again, welcome, and this is your home."

"Muchos gracias, amigo, ed Presidente de Mexico . . . ," Bush responded. "Thank you very much. It's a great honor to come to Mexico as this important nation enjoys a new birth of freedom, signaled by President Fox's election. Our meetings today have been a really good opportunity to renew our personal friendship and the friendship between Mexico and the United States."

Bush told President Fox that he looked forward to a future of freedom and prosperity throughout all of the western hemisphere. Together, they looked forward to the Summit of the Americas, a meeting of other leaders in the western hemisphere that was scheduled for the following April.

Following Bush's visit, Fox and his cabinet members stayed very busy. Francisco Barrio, who Fox appointed to lead his anti-corruption program, sent 700 auditors to look over the financial records for Pemex. The finance wizards discovered that company officials were marketing marine fuel as industrial diesel, a trick that was earning the company about $100,000 a day. By June, Barrio had also fired about 100 of the country's top customs officials and was cracking down on illegal imports from Asia.

There were other issues facing Fox, too. It was estimated that 465 members of Mexican groups who opposed the government disappeared between 1970 and 1982. Now that Fox was president and the PRI was no longer leading the country, families of those missing people began demanding answers. They asked that Fox establish a truth commission to investigate the disappearances and they wanted answers to their questions. It was a tough issue for Fox to consider. He agreed that the truth should be known, but he also knew that looking too closely at Mexico's past could bring his presidency to a premature end. The PRI still had a large vote in Congress and it could block any such investigation.

Fox's presidency was not easy. Some Mexicans criticized him because he traveled outside of the country too much. Others disapproved of some of his policy proposals. There was even a scandal regarding the amount of money that he spent on sheets and towels for the president's residence.

Still, there were some successes. In April, the Mexican Congress approved a law that would set up a new group of microfinance companies that could give loans as small as $50 to entrepreneurs. However, it would take months to write the regulations for the new loan program.

President Fox married his chief presidential spokesperson, Martha Sahagun, at a private wedding ceremony at Los Pinos on the morning of July 2, 2001. Fox and Sahagun were married one year to the day after Fox's winning the presidency; July 2 is also Fox's birthday. Some Mexicans were scandalized at their departure from strict Catholicism, as both were divorced. Both would seek annulments of their previous marriages in the months following the wedding.

With the July anniversary of his election coming up, Fox planned another surprise. One year from the date that he was elected, on July 2, 2001, he married his longtime spokeswoman, Martha Sahagun. The ceremony was held in private at the president's residence, Los Pinos, with only some family members attending. Now Fox had three reasons to celebrate July 2: his birthday, his election, and his marriage to Sahagun.

Fox wore a navy blue suit and cowboy boots and his bride was in an ivory silk suit as they kissed after the 8 A.M. ceremony. Even though it was known throughout Mexico that the two were dating, they never publicly discussed their relationship. Sahagun have moved into Los Pinos with the President after he was elected to office. Although it was a reported that they stayed in separate quarters, the arrangement proved to be scandalous to some Mexicans.

Sahagun, 48, was also a divorced Roman Catholic who was the mother of three grown sons and the grandmother of a one-year-old girl. She had been a volunteer on Fox's first, failed campaign for Guanajuato's governor in 1990 and continued to campaign for him in other elections. Fox appointed her his spokesperson in 1995, when he was elected governor of Guanajuato. At that point Sahagun was a university teacher who had extensive business experience. In 1994 she ran for mayor of Celaya, but lost. She was among Fox's staffers who, during his campaign, often wore jeans with FOX inscribed on a belt loop.

The president and his new wife seemed very happy with their decision to marry even though they broke away from their traditional Catholic religion by doing so. Because both Fox and Sahagun were both divorced, they were required to have their former marriages annulled, or excused, by the Catholic Church. The couple sought their annulments in the months after their wedding. Meanwhile, each practiced their devout Catholicism by attending mass even though they could not take communion in the church.

Following the wedding ceremony early on July 2, Fox proceeded with his usual business of being president. He met with the visiting Spanish Prime Minister who offered him triple congratulations for the day. Meanwhile, Sahagun stepped down from her official role as Fox's spokesperson to become Mexico's first lady. She was replaced by Francisco Ortiz, who had served as Fox's public opinion and image coordinator.

Sahagun was expected to be a different sort of first lady because of her experience in politics. She planned to be an active liaison between the government and private programs directed at women, children and those who lived in poverty. She studied former United States First Lady Hillary Clinton, who was elected a U.S. senator in 2001, and other such women to see how they handled their roles. Later that summer Fox allowed her to be his representative at the inauguration of the President of Peru. Then, in August, she met with other first ladies of Latin America while their husbands attended a Latin American summit in Chile.

The day after their wedding Fox gave a public speech called "Mexico Vision 2025 Initiative" at the National Museum of Anthropology. "Mexico Vision 2025 is a unique opportunity for us to set forth our dreams and make them come true, to exercise our freedom to choose the future we want," Fox said.

He continued with his speech, telling Mexicans that they must plan for the future because the success of their nation will be tied to that planning. He talked about housing, education, water, electrification, power, health, and communications.

"It will depend on whether or not we have strategic long-term plans to administer our natural resources, renewable and non renewable; on whether or not we plan our needs in communications, power, water, etc.; or whether or not we anticipate problems of public security, national security, employment, population growth, technological development; on whether or not we know where we want to go with our sport, our culture," Fox said.

It was important for President Fox to address the Mexican people one year after he had been elected. He wanted them to recognize that his administration was making headway into changes that Mexico needed for its future.

But by September many Mexicans were growing impatient about the changes that Fox had promised. They wanted to see results and they wanted to see them soon. Fox's first effort to

President Fox delivers his nationally televised State of the Nation address at the Mexican Congress in Mexico City on September 1, 2001. Progress in other areas of politics depended on Fox's long-awaited tax reforms.

create peace with the Zapatistas in Chiapas had weak results. Fox had won Congressional approval of an Indian-rights bill that was backed by the rebels. However, they rebels broke off all contact with the government after Congress amended the bill with provisions that the Zapatists disliked.

Many Mexicans also were disappointed with Fox's work to stop corruption, saying that the real crooks had not yet been found. Fox's plan for a truth commission had been put on hold. The tax reform that Fox had promised also had not yet occurred. Because reform was delayed, so were improvements for the country's education and welfare systems.

But there was hope. As one of its first orders of business, the upcoming Congressional session would study the tax reform issue. Working with Congress was not easy, however, since the PAN did not have a majority vote.

Even though some Mexicans were frustrated and there was even some disagreement among members of Fox's cabinet, the President continued to work toward his goals. One of his main goals was to work steadily with the United States to make changes regarding border policies and Mexican migration.

Fox hoped to make progress on these issues in mid-September during an official state visit in the United States with President George W. Bush. He and his new wife would travel together as dignified representatives of their beloved country.

President Fox walks with U.S. President George W. Bush, reviewing troops during an arrival ceremony at the White House on September 5, 2001. The successful diplomatic visit included essential discussion of immigration issues.

6

A Visit with President Bush

A twenty-one gun salute welcomed President Fox to the United States after his helicopter landed on the south lawn of the White House. Fox and his wife were greeted by U.S. President George W. Bush and his wife, Laura. A patriotic ceremony and a military parade kicked off the start of three busy days during which Fox would talk with Bush and other U.S. officials about many issues, the most important being a change of border policies to benefit more Mexicans.

"This is a recognition that the United States has no more important relationship in the world than this one we have with Mexico," President Bush told Fox in his welcome address. "The starting point of a sound foreign policy is to build a stable and prosperous neighborhood, with good relations amongst neighbors. Good neighbors work together and benefit from each other's successes."

On September 5, 2001, the partnership between Mexico and the

United States was at the height of its friendship. The North American Fair Trade Agreement had been in effect for several years, opening the doors for better business between the two countries and creating millions of jobs in Mexico that paid better wages. With NAFTA considered a success, the issue of migration of Mexicans into the United States remained a very important one.

Because many Mexicans still earn less than $2 per day and a large number still live in poverty, many aspire to work in the United States where they can earn $7 an hour or more. It is estimated that about 300,000 Mexicans cross the border into the United States each year to find work. An estimated three to four million Mexicans live illegally in the United States because they have not obtained the proper paperwork to enter the country. These people are called illegal aliens, because their entry into the country is not documented. Illegal aliens from Mexico have contributed to the largest number of illegal aliens living in the United States in the country's history.

When Vicente Fox's helicopter landed on the south lawn of the White House, the Mexican President knew what he had promised his countrymen during his campaign. Border issues between the United States and Mexico have long been discussed but Fox wanted to start some action on the issue.

The boundary between Mexico and the United States was established following the war between the two countries that ended in 1848. The Treaty of Guadalupe Hidalgo, which ended the war, was signed by both countries on Feb. 2, 1848. Among other things, the treaty established the Rio Grande River as the southern boundary of Texas, which had already become one of the United States. Mexico also borders the states of New Mexico, Arizona and California.

The Mexican border with the United States has long been protected by guards whose job it is to make sure that people crossing the border have the proper certification for either being a resident or a visitor to that country. Still, hundreds of

U.S. Customs inspectors open the trunk of a car carrying five suspected illegal immigrants in San Diego in September of 2000. Smugglers like the man who was driving this car have always been a problem for the U.S. Border Patrol, but illegal immigration is no less difficult to control. Many Mexicans, whose earning potential is low at home, emigrate in secret to the United States and then send money back to their families—an estimated $8 billion each year.

thousands of illegal Mexicans pass through the border each year.

"If you can make a living in America and you can't find a job in Mexico, family values don't stop at the southern border," President Bush said in a speech prior to Fox's visit. "People are coming to work to provide food for their families."

Many Mexicans who immigrate to the United States are faithfully loyal to their families that still live back home. It is estimated that each year they send $8 billion back to their Mexican families each year. Among President Fox's goals was one to set up programs to get successful Mexican immigrants to invest back in their homeland.

There was much pomp during the U.S. state dinner for President Fox, who was the first guest honored at a state dinner given by the new President Bush. Thirteen round tables were set with sage-colored tablecloths and centerpieces featuring white hydrangeas, roses and Casablanca lilies arranged around a base of fresh limes, which had been grown in Mexico. White and gold china was used by each of the 136 guests and the White House chef, assisted by First Lady Laura Bush, created a meal with a Mexican-American theme.

Prior to the meal, President Bush offered a toast to his guests. "This is not only a state dinner, it's like a family gathering. The most important ties between your country and mine, Mr. President, go beyond economics and politics and geography. They are the ties of heritage, culture, and family. This is true of millions of Mexican and American families, including my own. The Mexican People have changed and enriched America. Together, our nations are now working to strengthen the Americas. A long border lies between us, but it does not divide us. Nearly one million people cross that border every day; a quarter trillion dollars worth of trade crosses it every year. Because of the visionary NAFTA agreement of 1994, the trade between us crosses in ever greater freedom. That's a benefit to both our peoples, and a model to the world."

Bush's toast went on for several more minutes, then President Fox followed with a response. "I was recalling five years ago when we met at the Governor's Office in Texas (when Bush was Governor). You gave me a baseball. I don't know what was the purpose. Maybe you didn't see a future on your friend. At least in politics," Fox joked with Bush. "But I did see a leader. I did see a person which is very close to Mexico; a person that has in his heart, Mexicans, Mexican families. And of course, he's got in his heart his own people, the people of the United States."

The audience laughed at Fox's comments, as he smiled

toward his host. Both Fox and Bush are known for their good sense of humor. "So we not only have in common that we wear boots, Western boots. We not only have in common that we like to go to rest to our farms. We have in common that we like to see things happen," Fox continued. "And I learned to see President Bush as a man of action, as a man of word, and as a man of results. And this is what makes me sure, confident that we are going to build a future; that we are going to come up with answers to migration; that we are going to come with answers to confront organized crime on the international arena."

Fox strayed from his written speech and, as he continued to talk, the White House chef began to worry that his first course of the dinner would get cold before it was served. The first course that evening was Maryland crab with a stew made of spicy sausage, called chorizo posole. The main course was bison coated in crushed pumpkin seed with whipped potatoes and a bean and chanterelle ragout. But the meal ran only about five minutes late and those who were dining raved about the food.

Dessert was a mango and coconut ice cream dome served with peaches and a red chilepepper sauce, called tequila sabayon. It was decorated with hummingbirds and flowers spun from sugar. This was quite unlike a dessert that the same White House chef had prepared for a visiting Mexican president several years ago—an ice cream cake featuring a dozing Mexican boy in a sombrero leaning against his mud hut. The White House chef had learned after his last creation that his dishes should depict Mexico in a way that the country wants to see itself. To create a boy living in poverty in a mud hut was not politically appropriate.

After dinner, entertainment was in the White House's East Room featuring soprano singer Dawn Upshaw. Finally, at 11 P.M. guests were invited to the White House lawn for 15 minutes of fireworks, a display which caused some Washington residents to think that the White House was under attack.

Even though the first day of Fox's trip was a long and

Just before President Bush's visit to President Fox in February of 2001, members of the California Coalition for Immigration Reform, left, argue about immigrants' rights with unidentified college students, right, outside a federal building in Los Angeles. Members of the coalition are opposed to an amnesty for illegal immigrants already living in the United States. The plan that the presidents were discussing, to offer American citizenship to all illegal Mexican immigrants, found little support in the U.S.

celebratory event, business was on his mind. Back home in Mexico, some countrymen were not supportive of his trip to the United States. They thought that their president was spending too much time working on American issues when people in Mexico were suffering in poverty. Yet, other Mexicans recognized that it was important to have good relations with the United States, a country which buys the vast majority of Mexican exports and the foreign country responsible for creating the most new jobs in Mexico.

Immigration issues were at the forefront. When Bush was in Mexico six months earlier the two leaders had discussed providing blanket amnesty to the millions of Mexicans who had illegally entered the United States. That would have meant making all such Mexicans legal U.S. citizens, even though they had entered the United States without the appropriate paperwork. But that concept had little support in the United States. One reason was because other countries also wanted the same treatment for their citizens who had immigrated illegally into the United States.

Although President Bush initially supported Fox's attempts to legalize more than three million Mexicans, the idea was not supported by many of those in Bush's own Republican Party. Some people thought that members of Congress could be persuaded if provisions were made in the law that included English proficiency training, or the payment of a certain amount of taxes, or employment for a specified length of time.

Even though a survey taken by ABC News showed that most Americans did not support blanket amnesty for illegal aliens, some people thought that now was the time that immigration laws could be relaxed. Among supporters for relaxing the laws were the U.S. Chamber of Commerce, which represents businesses across the country, and the AFL-CIO, one of the biggest unions in the United States.

Part of that reason some people supported changes in the laws was because Fox was seen as the first legitimately-elected president of Mexico and because he was an honest leader with great business experience. Finally, Fox had plans to create more and better paying jobs in Mexico so that eventually fewer Mexicans would seek employment in the United States.

Because there was not much support for blanket amnesty, though, Bush and Fox revised their ideas. Bush proposed a revision of the guest-worker program that would allow thousands of illegal aliens, from Mexico and elsewhere, to get temporary U.S. visas that allow them to work in the United States. Currently, about 100,000 Mexicans get such privileges to work in agricultural areas of the country. But Bush proposed expanding the program to permit Mexicans to work in restaurants, hotels, and other such industries.

The two men had also discussed allowing more U.S. visas to be approved for Mexicans who were going to work for specific employers. Part of this plan would give Mexican workers some U.S. benefits, such as Social Security and the ability to take out insurance, get driver's licenses and other things. Joint patrolling of the United States-Mexican border and ensuring fair treatment of Mexicans who were living and working in the U.S. were also included in their discussions.

But immigration was not the only issue discussed. The two Presidents also talked about issues regarding energy, the environment and water; an agreement on food safety; a new scholarship program focused on economic development; and regional cooperation to strengthen democracy and prosperity in the Western Hemisphere.

On his first day in the United States Fox told Bush that he wanted a plan for immigrants by the end of the year, a statement that surprised Bush and his advisors. Fox was a man of his word, one who liked to see things happen. But changing immigration laws in the United States was not going to be an easy task.

Fifteen years earlier the U.S. Immigration Reform and Control Act of 1986 had allowed 2.7 million illegal aliens to be granted legal status. That Act had also had toughened border security and created a system that was supposed to deny jobs to workers who didn't have visas. But because the employment provision of that act was not enforced, Mexicans continued to illegally work in the United States.

The day after the elaborate state dinner, Fox appeared before a joint session of the U.S. Congress, supporting President Bush's request to Congress that there be a broad change in immigration laws. "Simple trust, that is what has been sorely absent in our relationship in the past, and that is what is required for us to propel and to strengthen our relationship in the days,

President Fox, second from left, makes a statement to reporters as President Bush, third from left, looks on during a bilateral meeting in the Cabinet Room at the White House on September 5, 2001. Fox would address a joint session of the U.S. Congress on the following day.

weeks, and years to come," Fox said during his address to the U.S. Congress.

In addition to talking to Congress regarding immigration issues, Fox also said he wanted to see the two countries cooperate on the enforcement of drug laws. Other issues that he discussed included an effort to crack down on money laundering from the illegal sale of drugs, speeding up of the movement of goods across the border, and possible plans to cooperate on energy ventures.

In a press conference with President Fox, Bush cautioned that immigration laws couldn't be changed too fast. Yet, some issues—such as family reunification and increasing the number of people allowed to get visas—were already being discussed by Congress. Still, there was much work to be done.

Immigration issues were some of Fox's key campaign elements that enabled him to defeat the PRI candidate, so the Mexican President was not about to give up. The next day Bush and Fox traveled to Toledo, Ohio, a city that has many Mexican immigrants. "I want to tell you not only that we love you and respect you, but that we need you back in Mexico," Fox told them.

Friday, Fox spoke before the Organization of American States, a group that represents 35 countries in the Americas, that was meeting in Washington. His topic concerned the 1947 Inter-American Treaty of Reciprocal Assistance, which focuses on military threats to any country in the Americas. Fox said that the treaty was outdated and that Mexico had a new vision for cooperation among the countries involved in the organization.

"Mexico proposes to be a principal actor in the discussion of a new system of security that strengthens the unity of our region, and at the same time permits us to identify and confront the true threats that face us," Fox said. "We don't confront an extracontinental enemy that obliges us to defend ourselves through a military alliance. We have, rather, common adversaries: economic backwardness and extreme poverty, organized transnational crime, the rupture of democratic legality and the systemic violation of human rights, the destruction of the environment, and helplessness in the face of calamities and natural disasters." Fox then offered to host a 2004 meeting of the OAS in Mexico.

Even though President Fox seemed to have made much progress during his visit to the United States, back at home in Mexico the economy was not doing well. Companies had scaled back production, causing more than 500,000 Mexican workers to lose their jobs. Mexico's problems were only reflecting the beginning of an economic recession in the United States.

Mexican voters, though, were impatient for the changes that their new president had promised that he would make in their economy. Fox had told them that he would create more than a million more jobs a year in Mexico, but with fewer U.S. companies making the move to Mexico during the recession that goal would not be met.

When Vicente Fox returned to Mexico on September 7, 2001, no one knew what the future would hold for his country's relationship with the United States and the rest of the world.

Smoke billows from the World Trade Center after two airplanes struck the towers in a terrorist attack on September 11, 2001.

7

September 11:
A Man of
Great Empathy

President Fox awoke early the morning of September 11, 2001. It had been only four days since he returned from his visit to the United States and he was looking forward to more discussion regarding immigration issues between the two countries.

Fox was scheduled to be the opening speaker at an event at Mexico's World Trade Center in Mexico City on the morning of September 11. But Fox's plans were interrupted when he heard terrible news regarding the United States. He was already at Mexico's World Trade center when he was told that airplanes had crashed into the World Trade Center in New York City and the Pentagon in Washington, D.C.

September 11 was the day that terrorists boarded four planes in the United States and caused all four of them to crash. Just before 9 A.M. Eastern Standard Time, two airliners flew into New York City's World Trade Center, which was known as the second tallest building in the United States. Minutes later another plane crashed into the Pentagon, the base of all United States military operations. A fourth plane, which officials believed was probably headed for another United States landmark building, crashed in rural eastern Pennsylvania.

The crew and passengers aboard all four planes died, as did thousands of innocent bystanders who were in their offices getting ready for the day's work. Thousands more people were killed when the World Trade Center fell after its structural base was weakened by the airplanes.

While Americans began to mourn their losses that morning, Mexico's largest telephone company experienced jammed phone lines as friends and family members repeatedly tried to reach relatives in New York City and Washington, D.C. Authorities evacuated the Mexican Embassy in Washington, D.C. that morning when many offices were closed due to the attacks on the nearby Pentagon. Flights between Mexico and the United States were cancelled—as were all flights entering and leaving airports in the United States. Mexican authorities were vigilant in attempting to determine if Mexican citizens died in the attacks.

Fox and leaders throughout the world were alarmed. The fact that terrorists could board airplanes and cause so many deaths in the United States left people around the world concerned for their safety.

President Fox called an emergency meeting of his cabinet members to discuss the issues regarding terrorism. Meanwhile, Mexico's federal police were called out to patrol the nation's southern border and to secure the country's airports. Police also performed security checks outside the United States Embassy in Mexico City.

President Fox took time out that morning to issue a consoling statement to President Bush. "I offer to you and the American people a show of solidarity and the feelings of grief of all Mexicans for the loss of life and damages caused," he said.

Fox also worked hard to assure that Mexicans throughout

Fox condemned the attack on the United States at a press conference on September 11, 2001 in Mexico City. President Fox wanted to pledge his and Mexico's support to the United States after the attack, but one survey reported that only one third of Mexico's people supported the alliance.

his country felt safe. He asked that Mexicans living in their home country, in the United States, and in other countries to stay calm. He told all Mexican consulates in cities throughout the United States to stay open throughout the ordeal so that native Mexicans would have a place to seek help. Once reopened, the Mexican Embassy in Washington, D.C., focused on those issues, too.

Prior to the disaster, Mexicans had been looking forward to annual celebrations held each September 15 to honor Mexican Independence Day. Those festivities were just a few days away and people in Mexican communities throughout the United States were looking forward to them. But immediately following the attacks, Independence Day celebrations in Texas, Florida, California and other states were postponed. The days after September 11 proved to be no time to celebrate.

Many members of President Fox's cabinet were on alert. On September 11, Foreign Relations Minister Jorge Castaneda was attending a meeting in Lima, Peru, with U.S. Secretary of State Colin Powell. Castaneda said he would immediately act in support of a United States' decision to seal the border it shared with Mexico.

Even members of Mexico's Congress expressed their sympathy for the United States. Many said they understood the possibility that the terrorist attacks could cause the border to be closed. The Mexican Senate met for only 10 minutes that day to pass a resolution that condemned the attacks and to express their condolences to the people and government of the United States. Governors of Mexican states that border the United States also vocalized their concern for their northern neighbor.

It only took about two hours in the early morning of September 11, it seemed, to jeopardize all of Fox's work toward creating a more open border with the United States. But Fox, like other world leaders, was ultimately concerned with thoughts of terrorism—in their own countries and in the United States.

Within days of the attacks, United States lawmakers started talking about hiring more border guards and changing the U.S. Immigration and Naturalization Service. Anti-terrorism proposals were being discussed by the U.S. Congress, including stricter immigration laws.

But, for Mexico, there was hope. Some United States lawmakers were determined that there should not be a backlash on border policies. Instead, they argued that existing immigration procedures needed to be examined to discover how the terrorists had entered the United States.

Six days after the attack, President Fox heard from his friend President Bush in Washington. Bush talked to Fox by telephone as he was attempting to build international support for a battle against terrorism. Talk of war dominated the news and the United States military forces prepared to head to the Middle East in search of Osama bin Laden and others who were thought to be connected with the acts of September 11. Instead of immigration reform, President Bush's agenda was now to form a coalition of support as the United States prepared for war in Afghanistan.

Back in Mexico, President Fox wanted to commit his support for the United States. While appearing on the "Larry King Live" show on CNN, in late September, Fox again expressed his support for the United States. But not all of Mexico's leaders felt that way. Their country had a long-standing belief that its interests were to be contained within its own borders. Some thought that Mexico should remain distanced from the United States' actions. They said that Mexico wasn't a country that fought in wars outside its borders. One survey showed that only one-third of Mexicans agreed with President Fox when he vocalized his support of the United States.

Mexico's policy of keeping its concerns inside its own border, perhaps, could be traced back to the mid-19th century war with the United States when Mexico lost nearly half of its territory.

Nonetheless, two weeks after the attacks President Fox sent a representative to a meeting of the Organization of American States in Washington. Mexico voted with other members to activate a hemispheric mutual defense treaty. Despite the fact that Fox, during his trip to Washington in early September, had told the OAS that Mexico would probably pull out of such a treaty. Now, though, times were different. It was time for Mexico to take a stand of support for the United States and its other neighbors.

After the terrorist attack on the United States, Mexican resorts usually popular with American tourists—such as this one, Cancun, shown over a month after the attack—were forced to lure Mexican tourists to fill their vacant rooms.

Mexico was tied to the United States in other ways, too. The U.S. economy had started to slow down several months before the September 11 attacks. Companies were closing and people were losing their jobs. This affected Mexican companies that exported to the United States. More than 500,000 Mexicans had lost their jobs when those companies scaled back in production. In southern Mexico, the recession coupled with the terrorist attacks affected tourist towns such as Cancun on the western border and Acapulco on the eastern border, where many people from the United States spent their vacations.

With the United States now focusing on better airline security due to the attacks, Mexican businesses were hurt even more. Transportation costs were increased and some people delayed or cancelled vacations because they were afraid to fly on airplanes.

Despite setbacks due to the terrorists attacks, Fox wanted to forge ahead on some of his other campaign promises. The three political parties in Mexico's Congress agreed that tax reform was needed. However, none of them agreed on the method to go about overhauling the tax system. Congressmen were deadlocked. Many of them disagreed with a proposal that had been made earlier by President Fox that sought to increase taxes. President Fox was anxious. If reform were not done before the end of 2001, he would not be able to start new programs he had proposed to improve Mexico's education and welfare systems.

Meanwhile, the terrorist attacks were still on his mind. Britain, Canada and some other countries had immediately supported the United States in its war against terrorism. But Mexico's low profile after the attacks put distance between it and the United States. Unlike British officials, Fox and other Mexican officials were reserved in their approach due to the country's past policies.

Still, Fox sought a way to repair the relationship. In early October, he traveled to the White House to meet with President Bush. Fox wanted to assure the United States that Mexico was a close ally.

On his way to Washington, Fox met with his cabinet advisors at a military air base less than a mile south of the United States border. Cabinet members updated him about work being done within Mexico in response to the attacks. There were tighter controls at airports; more intense border inspections; and increased security at dams, oil refineries, and electric plants. Fox then traveled across the border.

"September 11th really changed America," President Bush said as he welcomed Fox back to the White House. "President Fox understood that right off the bat. One of the first calls I got was from Vicente Fox. He called expressing his deep condolences to the American people. He was very kind to me. He wished me well. President Fox understands that an attack on America affects Mexico in a significant way. After all, there are millions of Mexican Americans and Mexican nationals living in America; men and women who saw a land they love attacked; men and women who have united around a great cause of defending freedom."

Fox thanked Bush for having him back at the White House. He expressed Mexico's sorrow for the United States, as well as its solidarity with the government and the American people.

"We are a friend, we are neighbors, we are partners, and we want to make very clear that this means commitment all the way, and that we will keep our commitments," Fox said in a public statement. "And we are working on an everyday basis, either in the border, either in customs, either in migration . . . on each of the subjects that have to do with security. We will be side by side in your efforts to defeat terrorism in the world and wherever it is."

Fox's October visit to the White House was quite different than the one four weeks earlier. The only time Mexico's President mentioned a migration issue during this trip was when he promised to cooperate in tighter border security. No one knew if, or when, immigration policies would be discussed between the two countries.

At that time United States lawmakers were introducing proposals that revised the system of getting a visa to visit the country. Other lawmakers proposed restrictions on student visas. Congress also wanted a better system to track foreign students attending colleges in the United States.

After Fox met with Bush, he traveled to New York City to meet with members of the Mexican community. By this time it was estimated that 15 to 20 Mexicans were lost in the rubble of the World Trade Center. The Mexican consulate's office in Manhattan listed 16 missing Mexicans, but others identified 23 people who were missing. The discrepancy may have occurred because some Mexicans were undocumented immigrants. The Mexican consulate in New York was also concerned because about 700 immigrants were now unemployed because of the collapse of the World Trade Center.

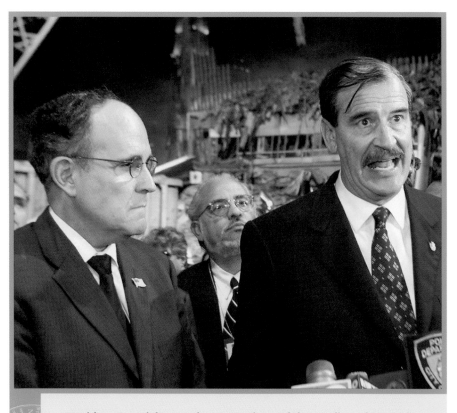

President Fox, right, speaks to members of the media as he stands with New York City Mayor Rudolph Giuliani at the site of the World Trade Center attack in New York on October 4, 2001. According to estimates, the attack claimed the lives of 15 to 20 Mexicans and left another 700 unemployed.

Meanwhile, in Mexico, there were efforts to help the victims. The Mexican state of Puebla set up a fund of $200,000 to assist the families of victims who may have come from that state. Also, one of the Mexican consulate's offices offered to pay for victims' families to travel to New York, if they needed to be there while awaiting news of their loved one. Families of illegal Mexican immigrants were having difficulty getting financial help from some of the other charitable funds set up to assist victims of the disaster. Illegal Mexican immigrants faced even more challenges during the turmoil because they were not official United States citizens.

In the aftermath of September 11, Mexico agreed to work with the United States and Canada to make the North American borders more secure. Mexico also agreed to align airport and airline security with new standards put into place by the United States. The Mexican government, under President Fox, announced that it would purchase new equipment to identify fake passports and plans were made to put a criminal database in place.

When the United States went to war with Afghanistan on Sunday, Oct. 7, President Fox gave his support during a televised address to his nation.

Just a few days later Mexico was given a seat on the United National Security Council. It was the first time in 20 years that Mexico was invited to sit on the council and many political experts thought it was a big success for President Fox. They said that the position on the council would provide another opportunity for Fox to express his viewpoint regarding immigration, drug trafficking, organized crime, and trade disputes. They also said that the position could make the president more popular in Mexico. President Fox said he was willing to send Mexican peacekeepers for missions of the United Nations.

Just a few days later, though, the PAN—Fox's political party—suffered a blow. Mexico's electoral commission overturned the mayor's race in the city of Ciudad Juarez, which is just across the border from El Paso, Texas. The federal group said that the PAN candidate, who was the incumbent mayor in the city, had won the election because he had unfairly used his advantage to influence the vote. Many people feared that the decision would hurt Fox's presidency. They thought Mexicans would say that the PAN and Fox were just like the PRI.

There were other issues that consumed President Fox's attention at this time, too. The same week the election ruling was made, Fox attended an international meeting in Puebla about microcredit programs. Finance companies from around the world were interested in opening offices in Mexico to offer small loans to poor people who wanted to start businesses. Already, some such programs were available in Mexico.

The war against terrorism and his other obligations did little to stop Fox from traveling. A few weeks later, President and Mrs. Fox visited Pope John Paul II in Rome. Because both of them were divorced, they did not visit the Pope together. Instead, the Pope first met with President Fox and then briefly met with his wife.

Even though times were difficult, there were lighter moments during Fox's presidency. He was the second Mexican president in history honored with a sculpture of his likeness that was unveiled at Tijuana's Wax Museum. The sculpture, created from 80 photographs given to the artist by Fox's staff and others, depicted the tall president in his legendary black cowboy boots stepping forward with a large smile across his face. Vicente Fox was only just beginning to make an impact on Mexico.

During a mass at the Guadalupe Church in Mexico City in memory of the prominent human-rights lawyer Digna Ochoa, killed on October 19, 2001, a nun holds up an image of the deceased. At the bottom of the poster is written "Digna lives; let there be no impunity." President Fox had promised to reduce the corruption of the Mexican government; because government involvement was suspected in Ochoa's killing, and because he had not heeded activists' pleas for protection, Fox lost support.

8

A President Trying to Stay Focused

T he first anniversary of Vicente Fox's presidency was fast approaching. It had been a busy year. Fox had visited the United States, Canada, and other countries. He had made proposals to Mexico's Congress. He had focused on border issues, and he had attempted to make progress regarding the crime and corruption in Mexico.

One year in office was not nearly enough time, though, to accomplish the goals he had set for his six-year term. Still, some Mexicans were impatient. They thought he was making no progress at all. The tragic events of September 11 had certainly slowed his work regarding border issues with the United States. Fox was among the many world leaders who saw some of his priorities change after the terrorist attacks on the United States. Being vigilant regarding terrorism and the safety of Mexico's citizens had become a priority.

Still, there were other prominent issues. Fox's presidency took a blow in October 2001 when a woman named Digna Ochoa was shot to death. Ochoa was a human rights attorney who represented many cases involving torture and murder in which Mexico's military and security forces were prime suspects. Due to a note left at the crime scene, there was no doubt that Ochoa's murder was related to her human rights work.

The murder of Digna Ochoa caused many Mexicans to feel that Fox had made empty promises. A government that was trying to eliminate crime and corruption would not have allowed such a thing to happen. Fox received criticism for not implementing a truth commission and for ignoring pleas for protection from other activists like Ochoa. He was also criticized for naming a former army general as Mexico's attorney general. In Mexico, the military for years has been accused of violating civil rights. It had long been suspected of executions, assaults, and disappearances of Mexican people who disagreed with the government.

Soon after Ochoa's death, Fox met with human rights groups and promised to investigate her death. Nevertheless, many people criticized his administration for not continuing its investigation into earlier crimes against Ochoa, including her kidnapping in 1999 and an assault in her home after that. After those incidents, Ochoa had left Mexico for a while but returned about seven months prior to her death.

Many people, including the United Nations high commissioner for human rights and the leader of the Zapatista rebels, condemned the murder. Some Mexicans living the United States requested that the U.S. stop providing training and funds to Mexico's military. Amnesty International and the Washington (D.C.) Office on Latin America were among the organizations that called for reform. Fox created a special commission to watch over the investigation of Ochoa's death.

In early November, Fox ordered the release of two environmental activists who opposed logging operations in the state of Guerrero. They had been in prison for more than two years. Some people believed their release was related to the criticism Fox received following Ochoa's death.

Because of the continuing corruption in Mexico, human rights groups urged Fox to take action so that the military would understand that crimes against citizens were forbidden. The Ochoa murder gave human rights activists reason to complain that President Fox was moving too slowly to clean up the corruption and crime in Mexico. Still, there were other Mexicans who remained in prison even though they claimed to have been set up by the government.

Other high profile crimes grabbed Mexico's attention during Fox's first year in office, too. In October, eight women were discovered murdered in the town of Ciudad Juárez, just south of the United States border. Fox ordered federal investigators to take over the investigation into the murders of 67 Mexican women who were found murdered in that town in the last eight years. Then, in early November two federal judges and the wife of a magistrate were killed in the town of Mazatlán. Those murders were thought to be related to Fox's strong stance against drug trafficking and organized crime.

Crime and corruption were only a few of the issues that haunted Fox's administration as it neared its one-year anniversary. Mexico's economy was still poor. The country had lost more than 200,000 jobs during his first year in office instead of adding thousands of jobs that Fox had promised.

Fox blamed his problems on the media, which in Mexico had been freer during his administration to criticize the president than in years past. Editorials and cartoons pointed out Fox's failures and guffaws, including his inappropriate etiquette of wearing black patent leather boots to a state dinner in Spain when he met with the king and queen of that country.

An unidentified man reads job descriptions at an employment resource center in Mexico City on July 23, 2001. Eight months after taking office on promises to create 1.4 million jobs, President Fox had actually *lost* 200,000; he fought to maintain public confidence in Mexico's struggling economy.

Fox told members of the media that they were attempting to ruin his presidency. There were even rumblings in Mexico's Congress about ways to replace the president. Congress failed to support Fox's proposed budget that predicted an increase in oil production and cut public spending. Fox attempted to put taxes on food and some medications. But congressional leaders, especially some who were members of the PRI, staged a public relations campaign against him. Fox was also criticized for having a high salary and for proposing a six percent increase in the salaries of all government workers. Fox said his salary and the salaries of others in his administration should be similar to salaries offered to people who work for big corporations.

Some members in Congress complained that the increase was inappropriate and that Fox's salary was too high in a country where so many people lived in poverty. Finally, Congress approved a budget that taxed soft drinks, telephone services, and cigarettes. Congress's version, however, raised less money for the government to spend on issues involving education and welfare.

Meanwhile, Mexicans even seemed to grow restless with Mexico's new first lady. Mrs. Fox established a charity called Vamos Mexico, which means "Let's Go Mexico," focused on raising funds to help Mexico's poor women and children.

However, the First Lady's first attempt at fundraising for the charity drew criticism. She invited Elton John to perform at a national monument in Mexico City called Chapultepec Castle. Some people said she should not have used the castle for the event. Others criticized her for taking a more active role in Mexican politics. Past first ladies had been more passive. She was frequently criticized for trying to be too much like U.S. Senator Hillary Clinton, a former first lady. They also said she was trying too hard to model herself after Eva Peron, an assertive first lady of Argentina during the mid-20th century who was featured in the movie *Evita*. President Fox attempted to defend his new wife's actions when the press started calling her frivolous.

Despite his troubles, opinion polls said that the majority of Mexicans still favored Fox. And, in a bit of comic relief during tense times, *People* magazine, a publication based in the United States, named Fox the sexiest world leader.

Criticism did not slow down, despite Fox's continued efforts to make connections with American businesses. In early November more than five dozen representatives from Los Angeles, Atlanta, and numerous other cities visited Fox in Mexico to talk about trade. A few weeks later, more than a hundred business leaders and the governor of Colorado visited with Fox. California's governor visited three weeks later with a group of sixty business and government officials. In between visits by the Americans, Fox also entertained the Prime Minister of New Zealand.

A break came for Mexico's president in mid-November when United States congressional leaders traveled to Mexico to renew discussions about immigration reform. Fox knew it would take longer to meet his goals, but he was glad discussions were resuming. Fox's cabinet had started revising their proposals in the aftermath of September 11. Officials pointed out that there was a distinction between foreign terrorists and poor Mexicans who illegally enter the United States to work. Meanwhile, President Bush emphasized the need for Mexico and Canada to work with the U.S. to secure North American borders.

The group also discussed economic development and security. Several weeks later, negotiators for the two countries reached an agreement that opened the U.S. border to Mexican trucks to meet the requirements of the NAFTA agreement.

Just before President Fox's first anniversary, he made a startling announcement. He said that the cases of more than 500 anti-government activists who disappeared in the 1970s would be more thoroughly investigated by a special prosecutor. Fox's comments came after he was presented a 2,000-page report created by Mexico's human rights ombudsman who was also the head of the country's National Human Rights Commission. The

November 27, 2001: President Fox, right, receives from Human Rights Commissioner José Luis Soberanes, left, a report of nearly 3,000 pages on the disappearances of political activists in the 1970s. The government's human-rights agency reported that 275 leftists had vanished while in government hands, and Fox's resolution to clarify the government's role in this and to compensate the victims was unprecedented.

president was also given names of dozens of officials, mainly police and security guards, who were suspects in the disappearances. The report was the first time that the Mexican government had admitted to having a role in the disappearances. Fox also announced the creation of a committee that would give compensation to the families of those who had disappeared.

Although many people criticized Fox's slow progress on his campaign promises, others pointed toward the good he had done. Fox had already started to tackle the issues of poverty and a tax system that favored wealthy people. He helped Mexico get a seat on the U.N. Security Council and improved the country's relationships with the United States. He made progress eliminating some organized crime and drug trafficking, although those problems still persisted. Some people said that Fox needed to focus more on just a few problems, instead of attempting to make a lot of changes at once. But Fox reinforced that fact that he had only three main goals: jobs, security, and human development.

By January of 2002, Fox was making progress on his goal to stop corruption. A special auditor found that $120 million had been taken from the government-owned Pemex oil. Investigators were trying to determine if the money was illegally used by the PRI party to support Fox's opponent, Francisco Labastida. Also in January an estimated 300 or more police were sent by Fox's administration to the peninsula of Baja to fight the war against drug trafficking.

"I have given clear signs with concrete examples of my readiness to face problems head-on, many problems that for many years were left behind," he said during an address honoring his first year in office. "Friends, I am a man of my word and I know how to keep my word—this is what I learned from my parents and I will keep my word to all of you. All the promises made during my campaign are being met. One year has not been much time to achieve the great objectives I proposed during the campaign. However, it has been more than enough time to show clearly that we are ready to guarantee the enormous changes that we wanted for our country, for our people, for our families, for our daughters and sons . . . The future is ours."

Meanwhile, President Fox buckled down to spend his second year in office focusing on Mexico's internal problems: its economy, crime, and poverty. He said he would not travel outside the country as much as he did during his first year and

President Fox, third from right, stands with legislators and other public officials at the National Palace in Mexico City on the Day of the Constitution, February 5, 2002. Fox renewed his call for a major reform of Mexico's constitution, suggesting re-election of legislators and changes in the adoption process of the nation's budget. In his second year in office, Fox promised to spend more time in Mexico, dealing with domestic issues such as crime and the economy.

that he would be more formal with the media. Still, some things never change. At a press conference when he talked about his new focus and formality, he wore a suit, tie, and cowboy boots. A year in office had not changed him much. Mexico's tall leader was busy looking toward the future.

1942

July 2 Vicente Fox Quesada is born, the second of nine children.

1964 Fox receives a business administration degree from Universidad Iberoamericana and begins working for Coca-Cola as a route salesman.

1971 Marries first wife, Lillian de la Concha. Follows with the adoption of four children.

1975 Becomes chief executive of Coca-Cola in Mexico.

1979 Returns to Guanajuato to work with his brothers in Grupo Fox.

1988 Fox is elected to Mexico's Congress for a two-year term.

1991 Fox's first campaign to be elected governor of Guanajuato fails.

He separates from his first wife.

1994 The North American Free Trade agreement goes into effect between the United States, Mexico, and Canada.

The Zapatista rebels take over part of the state of Chiapas.

1995 Is elected Guanajuato's governor.

1997 Announces his candidacy for Mexico's President's seat.

2000

July 2 Is elected President of Mexico.

2000

December 1 Is inaugurated into the presidency.

2001

July 2 Marries his second wife, Martha Sahagun.

September 5 President Fox is the guest of U.S. President George W. Bush.

September 7 President Fox returns to Mexico.

September 11 Terrorists attack the United States in the form of four airline crashes.

U.S. Congress immediately begins talking of tightening the country's borders.

October	Returns to the United States for a brief visit with President Bush. Human rights attorney Digna Ochoa is murdered in Mexico.
November	Talks regarding immigration issues resume with the U.S.
December 1	Celebrates one year in office.

Casagrande, Louis B. & Johnson, Sylvia A. *Focus on Mexico.* Minneapolis MN: Lerner Publications Company, 1986.

Fox Quesedo, Vicente. *A Los Pinos.* Mexico: Editorial Oceano de México, 1999. (Available only in Spanish.)

Kalman, Bobbie. *Mexico the Culture.* New York: Crabtree Publishing Company, 1993.

Kalman, Bobbie. *Mexico the People.* New York: Crabtree Publishing Company, 1993.

Meyer, Michael C. and Beezley, William H. *The Oxford History of Mexico.* New York: The Oxford University Press, 2000.

Oppenheimer, Andres. *Bordering on Chaos.* Boston: Little, Brown and Company, 1996.

Schlesinger, Arthur M. jr. *Juárez: World Leaders Past & Present.* Philadelphia: Chelsea House Publishers, 1986.

Abrams, Elliott. "Fox Populi." *The Weekly Standard*, July 17, 2000.

Allen, Mike. "An Unvarnished President on Display." *The Washington Post*, Sept. 19, 2001.

Anderson, John Ward and Moore, Molly. "Fox Brings New Style to Mexican Politics." *The Washington Post*, July 9, 2000.

Anderson, John Ward and Moore, Molly. "After the Battle, the Blood." *The Washington Post*, July 6, 2000.

Barone, Michael. "The New Mexico." *U.S. News & World Report*, July 17, 2000.

Berman, Paul. "Mexico's Third Way." *The New York Times Magazine*, July 2, 2000.

Bone, James. "Mexico's Plea to New Leader: Don't Fail Us." *The Australian*, July 5, 2000.

Borrus, Amy and Smith, Geri. "Spotlight on the Border." *Business Week*, Sept. 10, 2001.

Branch-Brioso, Karen. "Mexican Migration is Back." *St. Louis Post-Dispatch*, Nov. 21, 2001.

Brant, Martha. "Making Dinner." *Newsweek*, Sept. 17, 2001.

Carl, Traci. "Mexico's First Lady Launches Charity to Fight Poverty." *Associated Press*, Oct. 29, 2001.

Casagrande, Louis B. & Johnson, Sylvia A. *Focus on Mexico*. Minneapolis, MN: Lerner Publications Company, 1986.

Cearley, Anna. "Fox Sends Hundreds of Police to Fight Crime Near Border." *The San Diego Union-Tribune*, Jan. 23, 2002.

Cearley, Anna. "Fox Becomes a Museum Piece." *The San Diego Union-Tribune*, Oct. 20, 2001.

Chacon, Richard. "Mexico Victor Aspires to Cut Poverty, Graft." *The Boston Globe*, July 5, 2000.

Darling, Juanita. "Mexico's Landmark Vote." *Los Angeles Times*, July 3, 2000.

Dewar, Helen. "Deal Struck on Mexican Truck Access." *The Washington Post*, Nov. 29, 2001.

Dibble, Sandra and Cearley, Anna. "Fox Promises Mexico's Support of Terror Fight." *The San Diego Union-Tribune*, Oct. 4, 2001.

Diebel, Linda. "Mexican Presidential Hopeful Accused of Running Spy Army." *The Toronto Star*, May 17, 1999.

Dillon, Sam. "The Mexican Election: Man in the News." *The New York Times*, July 4, 2000.

Dillon, Sam. "From Moving Mexico's Cola to Shaking Its Politics." *The New York Times*, May 9, 1999.

Dillon, Sam. "Third in Mexican Polls, a Leftist Campaigner Manages to Project Optimism." *The New York Times*, Sept. 24, 1999.

Dillon, Sam. "TV Proves Most Potent Campaign Tool." *The New York Times*, Sept. 8, 1999.

Dillon, Sam. "Mexico's Opposition Party Selects a Peacemaker." *The New York Times*, March 7, 1999.

Dillon, Sam. "Early Bird Begins Mexico's 2000 Presidential Race." *The New York Times*, May 11, 1998.

Dillon, Sam. "The 'Sell Me' Politician the Mexicans Bought." *The New York Times*, July 4, 2000.

Dillon, Sam. "Mexico, Voting in New Leader, Begins a Political Sea Change." *The New York Times*, July 4, 2000.

Dolinsky, Lewis. "Notes from Here and There." *The San Francisco Chronicle*, Aug. 4, 1998.

Dominguez, Jorge and de Castro, Rafael Fernandez. "U.S.-Mexico Relationship on Solid Ground." *Newsday*, Sept. 10, 2001.

Ellingwood, Ken. "PAN Pioneers Went From Shadows to Day in the Sun." *Los Angeles Times*, July 7, 2000.

Epstein, Edward. "Mexico's Fox Wants U.S. Deal to Boost Standing at Home." *The San Francisco Chronicle*, Sept. 9, 2001.

Ferriss, Susan. "Mexico's Ruling Part Faces Test in Today's Vote." *Atlanta Journal and Constitution*, July 2, 2000.

Ferriss, Susan. "Fox Eyes Mexico's Presidency." *The Atlanta Journal and Constitution*. Nov. 27, 1999.

Ferriss, Susan. "Election in Mexico: Victor Vows to End Corruption." *The Atlanta Journal and Constitution*, July 5, 2000.

Ferriss, Susan. "Hope Sweeps Mexico as Fox is Sworn In." *The Atlanta Journal and Constitution*, Dec. 2, 2000.

Ferriss, Susan. "Variety Marks Mexico Cabinet . . . " *The Atlanta Journal and Constitution*, Dec. 3, 2000.

Ferriss, Susan. "Mexico's Fox Weds Spokeswoman." *The Atlanta Journal and Constitution*, July 3, 2001.

Ferriss, Susan. "Mexico's Fox Still Under Fire from Rights Activists." *The Atlanta Journal and Constitution*, Nov. 11, 2001.

Ferriss, Susan. "Mexico to prove disappearances." *The Atlanta Journal and Constitution*, Nov. 28, 2001.

Ferriss, Susan. "Facing Economic Hurdles, Fox Raises Nation's hopes." *The Atlanta Journal and Constitution*, Dec. 1, 2001.

Ferriss, Susan. "In Mexico, Barnes Hails Immigration." *The Atlanta Journal and Constitution*, Nov. 8, 2001.

"Fox Quesada, Vicente." *Current Biography*: May 2001.

Garza, Adolfo. "Mexican Governors Gather at Forum." *The News* (InfoLatina), Oct. 3, 1997.

Gerstenzang, James and Smith, James F. "Migration Issues Take a Back Seat in Fox Visit." *Los Angeles Times*, Oct. 5, 2001.

Gold, Matea. "Hahn Makes Bid to Build L.A.'s Ties to Mexico." *Los Angeles Times*, Nov. 6, 2001.

Gonzales, John Moreno. "Mexican President to Meet Victims' Kin." *Newsday*, Oct. 4, 2001.

Gonzales, John Moreno. "Fox Pledges Assistance." *Newsday*, Oct. 5, 2001.

Grayson, George W. "Marlboro Man and Fast Track Reform." *The San Diego Union-Tribune*, Sept. 9, 2001.

Hansen, Tom. "Despite Fox, Political Murders Continue in Mexico." *The San Diego Union-Tribune*, Oct. 25, 2001.

Hegstrom, Edward. "Lifting Barriers at Border Urged." *The Houston Chronicle*, June 16, 2000.

Hertzberg, Hendrik. "The Real Thing." *The New Yorker*, July 17, 2000.

Jacobs, Stevenson. "Mexico Offers Sympathy, Condemns Attack in the U.S." WorldSources, Inc., Sept. 12, 2001.

Jordan, Mary. "Fox Adopts More Formal Style." *The Washington Post*, Jan. 8, 2002.

Jordan, Mary and Sullivan, Kevin. "U.S. and Mexico to Resume Talks on Immigration Policy." *The Washington Post*, Nov. 14.

Kaggwa, Lawrence. "Fox's Win Viewed Favorably in Region." *The Plain Dealer*, July 8, 2000.

Kalman, Bobbie. *Mexico the culture.* New York: Crabtree Publishing Company, 1993.

Kalman, Bobbie. *Mexico the people.* New York: Crabtree Publishing Company, 1993.

Katel, Peter. "Fox's Game Plan." *Time*, Sept. 3, 2001.

Kraul, Chris. "Fox Proposes End to Energy Monopoly." *Los Angeles Times*, Nov. 1, 2001.

Kraul, Chris. "Fox's First Lady Sizing Up Her New Shoes." *Los Angeles Times*, July 5, 2001.

LaFranchi, Howard. "Mexico's Dynamic North Drives Change." *The Christian Science Monitor*, July 6, 2000.

LaFranchi, Howard. "New Rule Would Mean Presidents Are Born, Not Made." *The Christian Science Monitor*, July 1, 1998.

LaFranchi, Howard. "Trying to Renew Mexico a Handshake at a Time." *The Christian Science Monitor*, July 1, 1998.

Lindquist, Diane. "From Pop to the Top." *The San Diego Union-Tribune*, July 7, 2000.

Lloyd, Marion. "Mexican President Fox Weds Aide." *The Boston Globe*, July 3, 2001.

Lloyd, Marion. "Fox Makes Pledge to Mexico's Poor." *The Boston Globe*, Dec. 3, 2000.

Lloyd, Marion. "Mexico's Fox Frees Two Prisoners . . ." *The Boston Globe*, Nov. 9, 2001.

Lloyd, Marion. "In Mexico, Fortunes Go South . . . " *The Boston Globe*, Nov. 12, 2001.

Luke, Robert. "Fox's Savvy to Benefit Georgians' Trade Tour." *The Atlanta Journal and Constitution*, Nov. 6, 2001.

MacCharles, Tonda. "PM to Talk Security with Mexico, U.S." *Toronto Star*, Oct. 21, 2001.

Magnusson, Paul and Smith, Geri. "Between NAFTA and a Hard Place." *Business Week,* Nov. 6, 2000.

Malkin, Elisabeth. "The Toughest Job in Mexico." *Business Week,* June 18, 2001.

Mandel-Campbell, Andrea. "Hillary, Evita—and Now Marta." *Financial Times,* Oct. 13, 2001.

Mandel-Campbell, Andrea "Mexican Media's Love Affair With Fox Ends With Bitter Recrimination." *Financial Times,* Oct. 20, 2001.

Mandel-Campbell, Andrea. "Mexicans Attack Leaders Over Salaries." *Financial Times,* Nov. 15, 2001.

"Mexican War." *Children's Brittanica,* 1988.

"Mexico." *Children's Brittanica,* 1988.

Meyer, Michael C. and Beezley, William H. *The Oxford History of Mexico.* New York, N.Y.: The Oxford University Press, 2000.

Miller, Greg et.al. "Mood Swiftly Changes on Immigration." *Los Angeles Times,* Sept. 18, 2001.

Moore, Molly and Anderson, John Ward. "Opposition Candidate Wins Mexican Ballot." *The Washington Post,* July 3, 2000.

Moore, Molly. "The Selling of Candidates, Mexico Tries U.S. Way." *The Washington Post,* Nov. 4, 1999.

Moore, Molly. "Fox Sets Priorities for a New Mexico." *The Washington Post,* July 4, 2000.

Morain, Dan. "Davis in Mexico to Meet with Fox." *Los Angeles Times,* Dec. 3, 2001.

News Staff, "Fox Running Hard, Early in 2000 Race." *The News* (InfoLatina), Oct. 27, 1997.

News Staff, "Calderon: Gov. Fox Best for Presidency." *The News* (InfoLatina), Dec. 21, 1998.

News Staff. "The Man from Whom Miracles Hang." *The Economist,* Oct. 28, 2000.

News Staff. "Fox's political challenge." *The Economist,* Dec. 2, 2000.

News Staff. "The Fox Experiment Begins." *The Economist,* Dec. 2, 2000.

News Staff. "Bush, Fox begin U.S.-Mexican Summit." *www.cnn.com,* Feb. 16, 2001.

News Staff. "Fox's moment of truth." *The Economist*, Sept. 1, 2001.

News staff. "Mexico Can't Let This Chance Slip By." *Business Week*, Sept. 10, 2001.

News staff. "A Twist of Lime at the White House." *The Washington Post*, Sept. 13, 2001.

News staff. "D.C. Residents Blast Bush Over 'Big Bang.'" *The Houston Chronicle*, Sept. 9, 2001.

News staff. "Renamed Fiesta Now Scheduled for Oct. 26-28." *Los Angeles Times*, Sept. 21, 2001.

News staff. "Fox calls for freer flow of legal immigrants." *www.cnn.com*, Aug. 24, 2000.

Omestead, Thomas. "The big man from Mexico." *U.S. News & World Report*, Sept. 4, 2000.

Oppenheimer, Andres. *Bordering on Chaos*. Boston, MA: Little, Brown and Company, 1996.

Palmquist, Matt. "Mexico's New Leader was Quiet Kid Here." *Milwaukee Journal Sentinel*, July 10, 2000.

Perlez, Jane. "Change in Leadership is Welcomed . . . " *The New York Times*, July 3, 2000.

Peters, Gretchen. "Fox Falls Short on Tall Pledges." *The Christian Science Monitor*, Dec. 3, 2001.

Preston, Julia. "With Vote, Mexican Right Gives a Hand to Candidate." *The New York Times*, Sept. 12, 1999.

Preston, Julia. "Mexican Hotly Pursues Presidency." *The New York Times*, Oct. 8, 1999.

Preston, Julia. "Challenger in Mexico Wins, Governing Party Concedes." *The New York Times*, July 2, 2000.

Preston, Julia. "A Crowning Defeat." *The New York Times*, July 4, 2000.

Quinones, Sam. "Fox a true outsider in Mexican politics." *The Houston Chronicle online*, July 2, 2000.

Quinones, Sam. "Old Politics Ends New Journalism." *Los Angeles Times*, Jan. 13, 2002.

Reaves, Dick J. "Can Vicente Fox Save Mexico?" *Texas Monthly*, December, 2000.

Reuters news staff. "Mexican report blames federal agencies in rights abuses against activists." *The San Diego Union-Tribune*, Nov. 26, 2001.

"Revolution." Children's Brittanica, 1988.

Rockwell, Rick. "Fox Shocks the World." *In These Times*, Aug. 21, 2000.

Rodriguez, Rebeca. "Illegal Immigration Worries Most Texans." *Fort Worth Star Telegram*, Sept. 10, 2001.

Sanko, John. "Owens Visits Mexico's Fox." *Rocky Mountain News*, Nov. 14, 2001.

Schlesinger, Arthur M. jr. *Juárez: World Leaders Past & Present.* Philadelphia: Chelsea House Publishers, 1986.

Schrader, Esther. "Fox's Rise has U.S. Scrambling to Get Clearer View of What's Over Fence." *Los Angeles Times*, May 25, 2000.

Schwartz, Emily. "Mexican official seeks one currency with Canada, U.S." *The Ottawa Citizen*, May 23, 1999.

Sheridan, Mary Beth and Ellingwood, Ken. "Mexico Power Shift Extends to Legislature." *Los Angeles Times*, July 4, 2000.

Simpson, Anne. "The Allure of Clothes that Holler Freedom." *The Herald* (Glasgow), July 7, 2000.

Simpson, Amelia. "Improving Human Rights in Mexico." *The San Diego Union-Tribune*, Nov. 30, 2001.

Skiba, Katherine M. "Fox's Rustic Rural Ranch Says a Lot about His Heart." Knight-Ridder/Tribune News Service, July 16, 2001.

Smith, Elliot Blair. "Candidate pulls at Mexican Party's Grip." *USA Today*, April 5, 2000.

Smith, Elliot Blair. "Fox Has Historic Win in Mexico." *USA Today*, July 3, 2000.

Smith, Elliot Blair. "Fox's Historic Test will be Building a Coalition." *USA Today*, July 5, 2000.

Smith, Geri. "A Chat with Vicente Fox." *Business Week Online*, March 16, 1998.

Smith, Geri and Malkin, Elisabeth. "Mexican Revolution." *Business Week*, July 17, 2000.

Smith, Geri. "Vicente Fox, Executive Headhunter." *Business Week*, Dec. 11, 2000.

Smith, Geri and Malkin, Elisabeth. "Setting Himself Up for a Fall?" *Business Week*, Dec. 4, 2000.

Smith, Geri. "Mexico's Wagon is Hitched to a Falling Star." *Business Week*, Oct. 1, 2001.

Smith, James F. "Fox Vows Wider Probe of Past Rights Abuses." *Los Angeles Times*, Nov. 30, 2001.

Smith, James F. "Catholic Icon on Campaign Trail Riles Mexicans." *Los Angeles Times*, Sept. 18, 1999.

Smith, James F. and Ellingwood, Ken. "Fox Lays out Plan to Overhaul Justice System in Mexico." *Los Angeles Times*, July 5, 2000.

Smith, James F. and Kraul, Chris. "Mexico's Fox Faces a New Set of Challenges." *Los Angeles Times*, July 10, 2000.

Smith, James F. and Sheridan, Mary Beth. "Mexico's Landmark Vote." *Los Angeles Times*, July 3, 2000.

Smith, James F. "The Fox Visit." *Los Angeles Times*, Sept. 8, 2001.

Smith, James F. "New Treaty Idea Draws Positive Reaction." *Los Angeles Times*, Sept. 8, 2001.

Smith, James F. "Graft Probe Sets Off Political War." *Los Angeles Times*, Jan. 22, 2002.

Sterngold, James. "Legal Residency Hopes of Millions Dashed." *The New York Times*, Oct. 6, 2001.

Sullivan, Elizabeth. "Bush Woos Hispanics with Eye on 2004." *The Plain Dealer*, Sept. 10, 2001.

Sullivan, Kevin. "Mexico Reverses Triumphant Return of 'Tomato King.'" *The Washington Post*, Sept. 11, 2001.

Sullivan, Kevin. "Killing of Rights Lawyer Strains Fox's Credibility." *The Washington Post*, Oct. 26, 2001.

Sullivan, Kevin and Jordan, Mary. "Fox Takes Steps to End Army's Rights Abuses." *The Washington Post*, Nov. 10, 2001.

Sullivan, Kevin. "Fox Vows Prosecution of Rights Abuse Cases." *The Washington Post*, Nov. 26, 2001.

Sullivan, Kevin. "Thoroughly Modern Martha." *The Washington Post,* Sept. 4, 2001.

Sullivan, Kevin. "Mexico Acknowledges Role in Disappearances." *The Washington Post,* Nov. 28, 2001.

Sullivan, Kevin and Jordan, Mary. "Daschle, Gephardt Visit Mexico." *The Washington Post,* Nov. 18, 2001.

Tayler, Letta. "Oil Scandal in Mexico." *Newsday,* Jan. 25, 2002.

Tisdall, Simon. "Fox Should Not Count His Chickens." *The Guardian* (London), July 7, 2000.

Thompson, Morris and Rodriguez, Rebeca. "Mexico Ends Party's Reign." *Pittsburgh Post-Gazette,* July 3, 2000.

Thompson, Ginger. "Mexico President Installed." *The New York Times,* Dec. 1, 2000.

Thompson, Ginger. "Mexican Rebels Move Toward Peace Talks." *The New York Times,* Dec. 2, 2000.

Thompson, Ginger. "A Death in Mexico Symbolizes the Slow Pace of the Police Reforms That Fox Promised." *The New York Times,* Oct. 26, 2001.

Thompson, Ginger. "Rights Report Holds Mexico Responsible for Torture." *The New York Times,* Nov. 27, 2001.

Thompson, Ginger. "Congress Shifts Mexico's Balance of Power." *The New York Times,* Jan. 20, 2002.

Thompson, Ginger. "Mexico Wins U.N. Council Seat." *The New York Times,* Oct. 8, 2001.

Thompson, Morris and Rodriguez, Rebeca. "Fox Sworn in As New Mexican President." *Pittsburgh Post-Gazette,* Dec. 2, 2000.

Tricks, Henry. "Mexico may face pressure to set up currency board." *Financial Times* (London), Feb. 1, 1999.

Tuckman, Jo. "Images of Evita and Elton Trouble Mexican First Lady." *The Guardian,* Nov. 10, 2001.

Walker, S. Lynne. "New Era Begins." *The San Diego Union-Tribune,* July 3, 2000.

Walsh, Kenneth. "Broader Border?" *U.S. News & World Report,* Aug. 20, 2001.

BIBLIOGRAPHY

Warner, Gerald. "Bush Knows Where El Dorado Is." *The Scotsman Publications*, Ltd., Sept. 9, 2001.

Weissert, Will. "Fox Orders Inquiry into 67 Slayings in Juarez." *Associated Press*, Dec. 14, 2001.

Zarembo, Alan. "Taking the Reins." *Newsweek*, July 17, 2000.

Zarembo, Alan. "The Worst Job in America." *Newsweek*, Dec. 4, 2000.

Zarembo, Alan. "Mexico's History Test." *Newsweek*, July 2, 2001.

Zarembo, Alan. "An American Dream." *Newsweek*, Sept. 10, 2001.

WEBSITES

http://www.vicentefox.org.mx/

http://www.whitehouse.gov

http://www.elbalero.gob.mx/

page:

SHERRY BECK PAPROCKI is a freelance journalist who has written for the *Chicago Tribune*, the *Los Angeles Times Syndicate*, the *Cleveland Plain Dealer*, and many other publications. Her two most recent books, juvenile biographies about Michelle Kwan and Katie Couric, were published by Chelsea House in 2001. In addition, she has written and contributed to six other books for children and adults. A graduate of The Ohio State University School of Journalism, she lives near Columbus, Ohio, with her husband and two children.

ARTHUR M. SCHLESINGER, jr. is the leading American historian of our time. He won the Pulitzer Prize for his book *The Age of Jackson* (1945) and again for a chronicle of the Kennedy Administration, *A Thousand Days* (1965), which also won the National Book Award. Professor Schlesinger is the Albert Schweitzer Professor of the Humanities at the City University of New York and has been involved in several other Chelsea House projects, including the series REVOLUTIONARY WAR LEADERS, COLONIAL LEADERS, and YOUR GOVERNMENT.